# WHEN A PARENT
# IS MENTALLY RETARDED

# WHEN A PARENT IS MENTALLY RETARDED

edited by

## BARBARA Y. WHITMAN, PH.D.
Associate Professor of Pediatric
and Adolescent Medicine,
St. Louis University School of Medicine,
Associate Professor, St. Louis University
School of Social Services,
Director of Family Services and
Family Studies,
Knights of Columbus Developmental Center at
Cardinal Glennon Children's Hospital,
St. Louis, MO

and

## PASQUALE J. ACCARDO, M.D.
Associate Professor of Pediatric
and Adolescent Medicine,
St. Louis University School of Medicine,
Director,
Knights of Columbus Developmental Center at
Cardinal Glennon Children's Hospital,
St. Louis, MO

·PAUL H·
**BROOKES**
PUBLISHING CO    Baltimore · London · Toronto · Sydney

**Paul H. Brookes Publishing Co., Inc.**
P.O. Box 10624
Baltimore, Maryland 21285-0624

Copyright © 1990 by Paul H. Brookes Publishing Co., Inc.

Typeset by The Composing Room of Michigan, Inc.
Manufactured in the United States of America by
Thomson-Shore, Inc., Dexter, Michigan.

**Library of Congress Cataloging-in-Publication Data**
Whitman, Barbara Y.
    When a parent is mentally retarded / Barbara Whitman,
Pasquale Accardo.

        p.  cm.
        Bibliography: p.
        Includes index.
        ISBN 1-55766-028-X
        1. Mentally handicapped—Government policy—United
States.   2. Handicapped parents—Government policy—United
States.   3. Children of handicapped parents—Government
policy—United States.   I. Accardo, Pasquale J.   II. Title.
HV3006.A4W55   1990
362.3′3–dc20                                      89-34827
                                                   CIP

# Contents

# Contributors

**Pasquale J. Accardo, M.D.**
Associate Professor of Pediatric and Adolescent Medicine
St. Louis University School of Medicine
St. Louis, MO
Director
The Knights of Columbus Developmental Center
Cardinal Glennon Children's Hospital
1465 South Grand Boulevard
St. Louis, MO 63104

**Reverend Dennis A. Brodeur, Ph.D.**
Senior Vice President
SSM Health Care System
1031 Bellevue
St. Louis, MO 63117
Former Associate Director
Center for Health Care Ethics
St. Louis University School of Medicine
St. Louis, MO

**Joyce Coleman, M.S.**
Associate Director
Early Childhood Programs
St. Louis Association for Retarded Citizens
1816 Lackland Hill Parkway, Suite 200
St. Louis, MO 63146

**Noreen D'Souza, M.D.**
Assistant Professor
Department of Pediatrics and Adolescent Medicine
Department of Pathology
St. Louis University School of Medicine
St. Louis, MO
Director
Division of Medical Genetics
St. Louis University, Department of Pediatric and Adolescent
    Medicine
Cardinal Glennon Children's Hospital
1465 South Grand Boulevard
St. Louis, MO 63104

**Betty Graves**
7262 Hazelcrest
Hazelwood, MO 63042
Early Childhood Special Educator
Special School District of St. Louis County
Formerly Director of New Hope Learning Center and Parents
    Learning Together
St. Louis, MO

**David Graves**
7262 Hazelcrest
Hazelwood, MO 63042
Assistant Parent Coordinator
Parents Learning Together
St. Louis, MO

**Yvonne Haynes**
Developmental Therapist/Teacher
Early Childhood Program
St. Louis Association for Retarded Citizens
1816 Lackland Hill Parkway, Suite 200
St. Louis, MO 63146

**Kathleen Marafino, J.D., M.A.**
Parent of a child with a disability
Disability Rights Attorney
42 Middlesex Drive
Brentwood, MO 63144
President
National Down Syndrome Congress
Park Ridge, IL
Former Public Policy Fellow
Joseph P. Kennedy, Jr. Foundation
Washington, DC

**Gale Rice, M.S., C.C.C.**
Speech-language Pathologist
Clinic Director and Instructor
Department of Communication Disorders
Fontbonne College
6800 Wydown
Clayton, MO 63105

**Ursula Rolfe, M.D.**
Associate Professor of Pediatrics and Community Medicine
Co-Director, Pediatric Residency Training Program
St. Louis University School of Medicine
Cardinal Glennon Children's Hospital
1465 South Grand Boulevard
St. Louis, MO 63104

**Barbara Y. Whitman, Ph.D.**
Associate Professor of Pediatric and Adolescent Medicine
St. Louis University School of Medicine
Associate Professor
St. Louis University School of Social Services
Director of Family Services and Family Studies
The Knights of Columbus Developmental Center
Cardinal Glennon Children's Hospital
1465 South Grand Boulevard
St. Louis, MO 63104

# Foreword

The cause presented in this book concerns a problem for our whole society because it involves more than parents and the school, whom we generally think of as the primary caregivers for our children. The question is: *how well are children cared for in the homes of parents with mental disabilities?*

Fortunately, the United States takes a very enlightened attitude toward personal freedoms—everyone is free to conduct her or his life with as little governmental interference as possible.

Such guarantees, however, give rise to the ever present struggle between people coexisting in society and also the methods of compromise to use when there are conflicts between persons. Laws, in general, are not able to address every problem.

Citizens who have mental disabilities need to have the same guarantees of freedom as any other citizen. At the same time, citizens with mental disabilities must guarantee the larger society that they will also follow the laws established by our state legislature. Following these laws necessitates some degree of intellectual functioning.

There are some specific laws that place a burden on the parents of all children in society to ensure, for example, provision of shelter, food, clothing, education, and medical care. I think we would all agree that children deserve to have these basic needs met regardless of their parentage. A very obvious conflict arises when persons with mental disabilities exercise their freedom to procreate, yet do not have the resources to meet their children's basic needs as legally defined by our duly elected state legislature.

How then do we solve the problem of the right of persons with mental disabilities to procreate and raise children, and society's right to see that the children's basic needs are met so that they can become healthy, happy, and productive members of society?

I have been asked, "How can you remove a child from the custody of a parent before that parent even has an opportunity to care for his or her child?" The implication is that a parent who gives birth (mother) or is the acknowledged father has an absolute right to care for his or her child regardless of the situation.

The case law of Missouri, like that of many other states,

protects children by establishing a limit on this absolute right. Specifically, the standard in Missouri is that a child does not have to be killed or maimed before the court steps in to protect that child from potential harm. This is a vague standard, but at least it is some protection for the child.

Concerning the parents, the United States Constitution has been interpreted to give citizens the right to have children and then raise them. Further, the law of the State of Missouri, like that of many other states, also gives a child's parents preference in raising the child.

Parents with mental disabilities have different levels of ability and have become mentally disabled for different reasons. For example, a person may have a brain injury sustained at birth, or because of illness, or because of trauma. This person may have a nondisabled child who at an early age is intellectually superior to the parent. Without good supervision, an immature but intelligent child may have difficulties attaining the proper self-control that is necessary to grow up in a society that has laws by which everyone must abide. There are, of course, children with mental retardation born of parents with mental retardation. These children have special needs also.

The Juvenile Court does not see a large number of delinquent children of parents with mental retardation, but as we gradually increase our population of children from this type of family, the picture may become altogether different.

There has been an obvious increase in the number of children in foster care who are born of parents with mental retardation. Some children must be removed from their parents' custody at birth because the parents cannot understand the most basic instructions about the care of a newborn. Some of these mothers have been able to retain custody of their children because a family member or other kind person has taken the mother and child into his or her home to give hands on, 24-hour supervision to mother and child. Ideally, this is an excellent means of caring for these children. The problem arises when a second, third, or fourth child is born. Suddenly, the kind caregiver becomes overburdened.

The more difficult case for the court is a referral for neglect of a child of parents with mental disabilities. A typical referral comes from a hotline telephone call reporting that a particular home is incredibly filthy and without utilities and that the child is without supervision or medical care. The court may investigate along with a social worker from the State Department of Welfare and a police officer. The child may be removed by action of the social worker and the police officer. It would be the judgment of the social worker and police officer that the child was in a dangerous condition (likely to die or become seriously injured). The juvenile court then would issue a temporary custody order giving the child to the Department of Welfare. In the meantime, the police would call the Evidence Technician Unit to take pictures of the child and the home.

At the hearing or trial, the judge of the Juvenile Court has the difficult job of making all parties understand that the hearing involves only the child. The parents are not charged with any offense; the sole issue is the best interests of the child. Often I have found that lawyers do not understand this, and although appointed GAL (guardian ad litem) to represent the child, some lawyers still, as GAL, become embroiled in the arguments of the parents. (This happens mostly, I suspect, because the GAL's client is an infant and cannot communicate. Lawyers, by nature, always have to hear some argument.)

The argument in Juvenile Court, instead of being the traditional two-sided plaintiff vs. defendant argument, most often is two-, three-, or four-sided involving the State, the agency, the mother, the father, and the child. These are the parties to the action.

The judge, after hearing testimony and seeing other physical evidence, must make a judgment about the future of the child. Frequently, the approach has been to secure social work assistance for the parents with mental disabilities and ongoing supervision of the family by a social work agency so the child may be reunited quickly with the parents. This action does require an in-court admission by the parents that the "dangerous condition" found by the social worker, police, or court worker did exist and a promise that such a dangerous condition will not occur again.

If the facts are contested, the judge must decide if the dangerous condition did exist. In doing so, the judge would appear to be making some very subjective decisions about the mentally disabled parents' life-style.

Often these families are critically poor. They must live on welfare or have the most menial of jobs, making only minimum wage. All of the difficulties that attend poverty plague these families in addition to the added factor that they do not have the intellectual capacity to figure out ways to survive, such as where to go for assistance with housing, food, clothing, and utilities.

A word of caution, however, for readers. Remember that

the judge is not judging the parents and their ability; rather, the judge is trying to decide if the child can be harmed seriously in his or her home. The child is paramount; the parents are secondary. Often, judges are accused—as are social workers—of making judgments about low-income families' choices of lifestyle. I dispute this and prefer to regard my decision as that of a parent for a child. Is this little boy or girl safe and in a secure, loving environment?

It is very helpful if a judge who is making these decisions has a strong background in law, social work, psychology, and community resources. It is even more helpful to have GALs who have a thorough knowledge of these areas because the GAL can speak the language of the social worker or psychologist and can intensively search for family resources.

The GAL's role is terribly important because he or she may be arguing before an uninformed judge who has rotated into juvenile court and has little or no interest in this work and knows that his or her tenure on the juvenile bench will be short. The GAL who has taken the time to look into the child's history and the parents' history will probably have a greater intellectual grasp of the child's situation than any other participant in the courtroom. Superior knowledge of the facts is not only helpful in convincing a trial judge but is also helpful as ground work for the appellate court.

The avenues open to a GAL for inspection are numerous, including school records of both parents and child, psychological/psychiatric reports, hospital records (physical and mental), criminal and juvenile court records, social work reports, welfare records, Aid to Dependent Children records, social security, disability and employment history, and employer's records.

In conclusion, the juvenile court as a legal institution has a place in our community to resolve disputes. It is not necessarily a leader in establishing community standards or assistance to needy families. Law cannot solve all problems. I feel often we may only choose between alternatives that are not necessarily good choices for a child's future.

*The Honorable Anna C. Forder*
*Circuit Judge*
*22nd Judicial Circuit*
*State of Missouri*

# Acknowledgments

We extend our thanks for the support and contributions of many people. Foremost among those we should thank is the St. Louis Office for Mental Retardation and Developmental Disability Resources (MR/DD Office). The Office provided the initial support for the innovative idea to provide parent training for parents with mild to severe mental retardation. An initial grant was awarded by the MR/DD Office in July, 1983. This grant supported both a needs assessment as well as a pilot program. David J. Richter, Executive Director, represented the MR/DD Office and helped us over many seemingly insurmountable obstacles. The directors at the Knights of Columbus Developmental Center at Cardinal Glennon Children's Hospital and the New Hope Learning Center gave us time to pursue these ideas and listened sympathetically when we complained of beating our heads against bureaucratic brick walls. Our staff included David Graves, Yvonne Haynes, Gail Rice, Darlene Kucera, JoAnn Hamilton, Susan Harding, Margaret Mills, Jeff Caul and others. As the program grew, we received both solicited and unofficial support from multiple agencies: the St. Louis Regional Center, Mike Haynes at the City Juvenile Court, the Missouri Division of Family Services, and the Visiting Nurse Association. Spouses, including Al Graves and Bud Whitman, volunteered to paint walls, move furniture, and make toys. Many church youth groups collected clothes and children's furniture. When the editors were no longer able to continue the program, it was implemented by the current program managers of the St. Louis Association for Retarded Citizens and continued to be funded by the MR/DD Office.

Again, our thanks to the St. Louis Office for Mental Retardation and Developmental Disability Resources and the Productive Living Board of St. Louis County for use of the "Right to be Proud" public awareness promotional material in the opening chapter. Finally, Columbian Charities of Missouri supported the editors throughout the 6 years of work reflected in this volume.

This book is dedicated to
the Missouri Knights of Columbus,
who, through Columbian Charities,
have generously supported our work
with mentally retarded persons
over the past 8 years.

# WHEN A PARENT
# IS MENTALLY RETARDED

# I Introduction

# 1 || Mentally Retarded Parents in the Community

Barbara Y. Whitman
Pasquale J. Accardo

Picture: A young girl with Down Syndrome is stirring bubble mix, then blowing bubbles; a bubble bursts.

Voice: Ginny is mentally retarded; she may be a neighbor of yours now, but where will she live when she grows up and her parents are gone? Ginny may face a harsh reality when the bubble bursts.

Picture: A Down Syndrome woman bewildered, sad, slowly stirring a bowl of cake batter.

Voice: That's sad, because today, people like Ginny learn how to live and work in the community, in real homes in real neighborhoods. Wouldn't she be happiest in a nice neighborhood like yours? Like the one she grew up in? It's just human decency. It's also part of her "Right to be Proud." (St. Louis Office For Mental Retardation and Developmental Disability Resources, Productive Living Board of St. Louis County.)

This public service announcement is one in an ongoing series in a community awareness campaign to highlight the needs of persons with mental retardation. This particular announcement underscores the contradictory societal attitudes surrounding adults with mental retardation. The effort toward deinstitutionalization and normalization is met by a "not in my neighborhood" backlash. The editors of this book were aware of these attitudes but were unprepared for the intensity of negative responses when the subject of adults with mental retardation as parents was addressed. This book reflects the first 6 years of a journey with these adults. That journey has brought accusations of religious doctrinal effetism from journal editors wanting to avoid this sticky issue, resulted in charges of amorality and ethical satanism from religious leaders, produced stonewalling and closed ears on the part of state and federal funding sources, and brought demands for *markedly increased services* from local social service agencies whose clients have benefited from the programming described.

The editors are directors of a multidisciplinary, privately funded developmental disabilities clinic. In the early 1980s, routine evaluation of a 30-month-old girl revealed markedly *depressed* language with above average nonverbal problem solving skills. Her mother was 40 years old, recently deinstitutionalized, and had severe to moderate mental retardation. An observation of the ongoing parent-child interaction led us to note that the 30-month-old daughter was already, in many ways, assuming the parenting function for her own mentally retarded mother. Yet, we also observed a bonding between mother and child that was positive. This led us to question how best to program for this family.

As our interest in this issue became known, more such individual situations were referred, and "horror stories" began to emerge. Adults with mental retardation are very literal, so when directions are given to them they often follow the directions relentlessly. Thus, when a physician told a mother who had mental retardation to place her child on clear liquids, yet failed to tell her when to discontinue them, the mother followed the instructions literally, and the child was admitted 3 weeks later for failure to thrive. Much to the mother's confusion, her parental rights were eventually terminated. Other stories of this sort were not uncommon. As adults with mental retardation tried to be parents, society inadvertently double-crossed them. Equally striking was the impression that these parents' situations were not rare.

Thus our journey was launched. The St. Louis Office for Mental Retardation and Developmental Disability Resources funded an initial epidemiological survey to determine the extent of the situation and a concurrent pilot project to conduct a parenting program and develop a curriculum for 10 families. This book is the culmination of those efforts.

## THE BIRTH OF AN IDEA

As we planned the initial program we continually ran headlong into legal issues (e.g., what constitutes informed consent when the signer has mental retardation), religious/ethical issues (e.g., whether or not natural birth control can be taught to a person who cannot count to 28), medical issues (e.g., dental and hearing emergencies), and system failures (e.g., lack of transportation funds for nonproductive adults). The published literature offered little guidance.

Yet, mentally retarded adults in the community are marrying and/or having children. (Earlier reports on the quality and duration of marriages involving adults who have mental retardation seem less relevant to issues of parenting in the presence of an increasing number of single parent families [Berry & Shapiro 1975, Mattinson 1971, Shaw & Wright 1960].) Previous attempts to teach mentally retarded adults parenting skills have been limited to programs such as modified Red Cross Baby Sitter's courses, which focus on emergency situations (Madsen, 1979); more general parenting skills training programs aimed at neglectful and abusive parents, some of whom happen to have mental retardation (Rosenberg & McTate, 1982); and behavior modification research paradigms (Feldman, 1986; Hudson, 1982; Peterson, Robinson & Littman, 1983). The optimism expressed by narrow-based research programs (Feldman, Case, Towns, & Betel, 1985; Feldman et al., 1986) is not supported in the real world, for our population included more persons with moderate to severe mental retardation. In the clinical experience of many professionals, the pessimism of a previous generation (Michelson, 1947) receives daily reinforcement. The purpose of this book is to attempt to steer a middle course between the unrealistically high expectations of the laboratory researcher and the burnout of the front line social services provider.

The chapters on the medical perspective highlight two major conclusions. First, from a genetic standpoint, most children of parents with mental retardation do not have mental retardation themselves. Mental retardation does occur in this group of children at a higher rate than in the general population, but in close to half those instances, mental retardation is secondary to environmental deprivation. Second, the health care needs of children whose parents have mental retardation are at significant risk of severe neglect. The chapters on epidemiology suggest that adults in the community who have mental retardation are having children at a rate comparable to that of childbearing in the general population with no suggestion of any IQ dependent differential fertility rate. Also noted are many indicators of complete failure on the part of the existing social service and other support networks to even begin to meet the needs of this high-risk population. The chapters on educational intervention record the experiences of two affiliated programs combining center-based and in-home parent training components. In the day-to-day management of these programs the true complexity and magnitude of the situation are best revealed. It would be both simplistic and unfair to summarize this mixture of successes and failures as reflecting merely that IQ was not the sole predictor of outcome. The chapters on legality and ethics review the rights of adults with mental retardation to marry and have children, as well as the potential conflict of those rights with children's rights to adequate parenting. Good ethics presume accurate facts; the limited data base in this area makes valid ethical conclusions extremely problematical.

Not all the contributors to this volume agree with each other. Not all the contributors to individual chapters agree among themselves. (The editors disagree on such issues as abortion, abortion of abnormal fetuses, sterilization of persons with mental retardation and the rights of persons with mental retardation to marry.) But the parenting issues raised are relatively new; the social setting in which they are raised continues to be a rapidly changing one. Potential solutions demand a level of social responsibility that does not appear probable. A limited number of available responses will make necessary choices seem that much harder. Any rational public discussion of this situation demands that the terms of the debate be clearly defined and consistently adhered to.

## MISDIAGNOSING THE PROBLEM

In the late 1970s the American Association on Mental Deficiency (AAMD [now the American Association on Mental Retardation (AAMR)]) changed the definition of mental retardation to require *significantly* subaverage general intellectual functioning. The IQ cut off for mental retardation was thus shifted from one standard deviation below the mean (approximately 85 on most standardized tests) to two standard deviations below the mean (approximately 70 on most standardized tests). As a result, the category of borderline mental retardation disappeared, and the theoretical prevalence of mental retardation declined from 16% to less than 3% of the general population (Blatt, 1987).

IQ scores between 70 and 85 can accurately measure cognitive limitations that both contribute to and are a reflection of limitations in learning ability and educational and employment opportunities, and isolation in terms of social class. Nevertheless, it represents a serious misuse of mental retardation terminology to persistently report intervention programs with both mentally retarded children and retarded adults who have mental retardation when the IQ scores reveal that half or more of these persons did not meet minimal psychometric criteria for mental retardation. The professional literature betrays a consistent bias in terms of placing high credibility on program outcome data that exhibit a positive trend (while exercising little criticism of the accuracy of the input criteria). Negative outcome data typically precipitate a much more stringent application of rigorous subject selection and research design criticism. This confusion contributes to serious difficulties in the area of public policy. Much of the literature on parents with mental retardation accurately describes the problems with parenting noted in parents within the IQ range of 75–80, now known as borderline intelligence, and combinations of parents with borderline intelligence and mild mental retardation. The application of results relevant to borderline mental retardation to adults with IQ scores more solidly in the 50–70 range or lower remains problematical. An IQ score in the borderline range cannot be considered presumptive evidence of parental incompetence, of the need for increased support services, or of extenuating circumstances for severely inadequate parenting.

Reports of successful intervention strategies for improving the parenting skills of adults with milder cognitive limitations suggest that the problems of parents with mental retardation are amenable to mild to moderate levels of social support services. The qualification that such studies do not say anything about the potential parenting skills of adults who have more severe mental retardation begs the question.

The current literature on parents with mental retardation is seriously flawed on other grounds. There appears to be little sensitivity to the increased prevalence of a wide variety of other disabilities in the population being reported. After potentially misclassifying adults with mental retardation by IQ or a "social needs" definition, there is little to suggest that impairments in vision and hearing or the presence of major psychiatric diagnoses are being routinely explored as either associated disabilities to the central disability of mental retardation or as confounding factors that would invalidate any diagnosis of mental retardation in the first place. Even the ominous qualifier "previously institutionalized" can mask an extremely heterogeneous population with a mean full scale IQ of 76 (range 53–110) and a significant subgroup of emotionally disturbed individuals who do not have mental disability (Floor, Baxter, Rosen, & Zisfein, 1975). Finally, learning disabilities and language disorders are among the most common developmental diagnoses in children. As neurodevelopmental disabilities, they are lifelong disorders with complex presentations in adulthood. Yet human service professionals who work exclusively with adult populations seem to be unaware of the ways in which such disorders can mimic both the cognitive and social dysfunctions that occur in persons with mental retardation. In the clinical case material described in this book, parents who were noted to have severe learning disabilities, language disorders, hearing or vision impairments, and psychiatric diagnoses, but who did not have mental retardation, were excluded; adults with these disorders who also had mental retardation were included. The differentiation between these two groups was not always easy or made early and may still not be complete.

Again, it is imperative that the contents of this volume be interpreted within the proper perspective. While the presence of minimal crossover cannot be entirely excluded, the mentally retarded parents discussed in the present work were at levels of functioning entirely different from those of the experimental subjects in such programs as Heber's Milwaukee Project and Ramey's Abecedarian Project (Spitz 1986). The experiences discussed in this volume focus on parents with mental retardation who do not accurately remember their child's birthday; who subtract backwards from their own current age to estimate when their child walked; who, with several children in the family, cannot recall all their names or consistently distinguish one child from another; who have trouble putting their toddler's shoes on the correct feet. A three-meal-a-day routine; a normal sleep wake cycle; safe, supervised, structured play; verbal interactions; following prescribed medication regimens—none of these situations is to be assumed in this population.

In the 1930s a number of papers came out of the University of Iowa Child Research Station that purported to demonstrate that severely mentally disabled ("retarded") infants and young children could show dramatic improvements in IQ when placed in the care of institutionalized mentally retarded ("feeble-minded") women (e.g., Skeels & Dye, 1939). Although the present clinical material has not made any attempt to document IQ changes in the children over time, our observations support significant limitations with regard to parenting on the part of adults with mental retardation. Such limitations are open to intervention strategies in the preschool years in selected cases but would appear to be much less remediable in the case of older children. In the absence of a commitment from society to provide an intensity of support services for parents who have mild to moderate mental retardation, the rights of children to a minimal expected parenting competence may need to severely restrict the rights of parents with mental retardation. If adequate parenting is a child's right, it becomes an adult's duty. There cannot be separate standards (Fotheringham, 1971).

## REFERENCES

Berry, J.D., & Shapiro, A. (1975). Married mentally handicapped patients in the community. *Proceedings of the Royal Society of Medicine, 68,* 795–798.

Blatt, B. (1987). *The conquest of mental retardation.* Austin, Texas: Pro-Ed.

Feldman, M.A. (1986). Research on parenting by mentally retarded persons. *Psychiatric Clinics of North America, 9,* 777–796.

Feldman, M.A., Case, L., Towns, F., & Betel, J. (1985). Parent education Project I: The development and nurturance of children of mentally retarded parents. *American Journal of Mental Deficiency, 90,* 253–258.

Feldman, M.A., Towns, F., Betel, J., Case, L., Rincover, A., & Rubino, C.A. (1986). Parent Education Project II: Increasing stimulating interactions of developmentally handicapped mothers. *Journal of Applied Behavior Analysis, 19,* 23–37.

Floor, L., Baxter, D., Rosen, M., & Zisfein, L. (1975). A survey of marriages among previously institutionalized retardates. *Mental Retardation, 13,* 33–37.

Fotheringham, J.B. (1971). The concept of social competence as applied to marriage and child care in those classified as mentally retarded. *Canadian Medical Association Journal, 104,* 813–816.

Hudson, A.M. (1982). Training parents of developmentally handicapped children: A component analysis. *Behavior Therapy, 13,* 325–333.

Madsen, M.K. (1979). Parenting classes for the mentally retarded. *Mental Retardation, 17,* 195–196.

Mattinson, M.J. (1971). *Marriage and mental handicap.* Pittsburgh: University of Pittsburgh Press.

Michelson, P. (1947). The feebleminded parent: A study of 90 family cases. *American Journal of Mental Deficiency, 51,* 644–653.

Peterson, S.L., Robinson, E.A., & Littman, I. (1983). Parent child interaction training for parents with a history of mental retardation. *Applied Research in Mental Retardation, 4,* 329–342.

Rosenberg, S.A., & McTate, G.A. (1982). Intellectually handicapped mothers: Problems and prospects. *Children Today, 11,* 24–26.

Shaw, C.H., & Wright, C.H. (1960). The married mental defective: A follow-up study. *Lancet, 1,* 273–274.

Skeels, H.M., & Dye, H.B. (1939). A study of the effects of differential stimulation on mentally retarded children. *Journal of Psycho-Asthenics, 44,* 114–136.

# II Epidemiological Perspectives

# 2 Epidemiological Probes

## Agency surveys and needs assessment questionnaires

Barbara Y. Whitman
Pasquale J. Accardo

The true prevalence of parents with mental disabilities is unknown and possibly unknowable. A sound epidemiologic survey to make such a determination is fraught with methodological difficulties and other barriers. Nevertheless, some attempt to estimate the magnitude of this situation represents a necessary first step in moving toward a solution. Chapter 2 describes the results of two preliminary epidemiological probes conducted in the greater St. Louis area. The first study focused on the city of St. Louis and was supported by a grant from the St. Louis Office for Mental Retardation and Developmental Disabilities Resources (Whitman, Graves, & Accardo, 1987). The second focused on the county of St. Louis and was funded by a grant from the Productive Living Board of St. Louis County. Although contiguous geographically, the composition and population of these two areas are markedly disparate. The problems encountered in conducting these surveys are described for the purpose of facilitating future studies and to help qualify the impact of the data. Preliminary findings with regard to life stresses and child problems are also discussed from the perspectives of both the parents with mental retardation and the involved agency professionals.

## STUDY METHODOLOGY

The most accurate method of determining the *actual number* of parents who have mental retardation would include a door-to-door census and *prevalence* determination with validating testing, or a universe sampling strategy such as that employed by the Epidemiologic Catchment Area (ECA) project at the National Institute of Mental Health (NIMA) in their effort to determine the number of persons with *mental illness* in the population (e.g., Klerman, 1986). Clearly this is not a practicable methodology for a number of reasons. A more practical alternative is to determine the number of parents with mental retardation who come to agency attention. This is known as the "Key Informant" method (Tremblay, 1957). It has two inherent weaknesses, however: 1) a tendency to *underestimate* the actual number of targeted people in the population under study since not all of any subpopulation will come to agency attention, and 2) a slight *bias* in the sample in that those who do come to agency attention may be a more problematic population (Warheit, Buhl, & Bell, 1978). Both limitations of this methodology might be lessened when the target is the population of persons with mental retardation since, by virtue of their disability, most of this population will at one time or another probably seek help through a service or other government agency. However, even in this population this methodology can be expected to yield somewhat of an underestimate in that a number of these adults will, for various reasons, escape agency attention. This is particularly true for those adults who did not receive services under PL 94-142 (The Education for All Handicapped Children Act, 1975) or other government programs. And the Key Informant method can yield a somewhat biased sample from this population in that those who are not currently receiving any agency services are likely to be those adults who are cognitively higher functioning and have solid family support systems. Furthermore, there is an understandable reluctance among professionals in the field to set up lifelong classification registries. (Potential sources of bias are outlined in Tables 2.1, 2.2, 2.3.) Despite these limitations, the Key Informant method offers the best access to, and the most economic and efficient way for determining the number of, parents who

Table 2.1.   Client factors contributing to underreferral

Better verbal rote sequential skills masking underlying cognitive limits

Splinter skills masking underlying cognitive limits

Superior social and life skills training

Limited interaction with agency professionals (e.g., food stamps service provider)

Spouse who does not have mental retardation

Effectively supportive extended family

Child neglect

Child abuse

Child sexual abuse

Ethnic background opposed to utilizing existing service network

Induced fear of utilizing existing service network

have mental retardation, their everyday level of functioning, and their problems with their children.

The survey was conducted in two stages: 1) an agency informant method was used to identify a sample of parents who had mental retardation in the community, and 2) a subset of identified parents with mental retardation was screened and interviewed to validate the referrals and to obtain the survey information sought concerning parental needs. In determining the service needs of these clients, these two stages are methodologically known as the key informant and the identified client, respectively.

Table 2.2.   Client factors contributing to overreferral

Hearing impairment

Severe learning disability

Language disorder

Articulation problem

Depression

Psychosis

Alcoholism

Substance abuse

Functional illiteracy

Educational deprivation

Severe chronic sociocultural deprivation

Borderline intelligence, complicated by one or more of the above

Table 2.3.  Agency factors contributing to over/underreferral

Inability to classify/diagnose
Refusal to classify/diagnose
Unavailability of previous records
Difficulties in obtaining previous records
Consent issues relating to obtaining previous records or per-
 forming testing
Professional competence
Professional sensitivity
Inadequate funding for assessment
Inadequate professional expertise for assessment
Staffing shortages
Incorrect/incomplete records
Child misdiagnosis

## STUDY ONE: ST. LOUIS CITY

### Stage 1: Key Informant

In order to facilitate the selection of agencies serving clients for Study One in the city of St. Louis, and to ensure as broad an agency sampling as possible in Stage 1, an eight-member advisory board (representing regional funding for provision of service providers, agency directors, and the researchers) was convened to: 1) identify all agencies that might serve or know of parents with mental retardation who reside in the St. Louis city area, 2) review the interview process, and 3) help to specify the type and range of questions to be asked in the parent survey. Two meetings of the board helped to identify those agencies and specify the questions to be asked about all identified clients. As an initial strategy, a letter of introduction to the study was sent to all agency directors. This letter described the purpose of the study and noted that someone from the project would be calling them within the week to further discuss their participation.

Initially 79 agencies were contacted. Over the course of the study, an additional eight agencies were added for a total of 87 agencies contacted (Table 2.4). In the telephone interview that followed, 35 agencies (40%) agreed to participate in the study. The other 52 (60%) agencies declined participation for various reasons. The reason cited most frequently was that there was no way to retrieve relevant data from their files. Following their agreement to participate in the study, all participating agen-

Table 2.4.    Number of agencies contacted to identify retarded parents
($N = 81$)

| Type of agency | Contacted | Participating | Identifying one or more adults |
|---|---|---|---|
| Handicapping condition agencies[a] | 10 | 5 | 5 |
| Hospitals | 10 | 8 | 5 |
| Medical clinics | 14 | 6 | 5 |
| Counseling agencies | 9 | 3 | 1 |
| Sheltered workshops | 8 | 6 | 3 |
| Women's shelters[b] | 11 | 5 | 4 |
| Birth counseling agencies | 5 | 0 | 0 |
| Crisis hotlines | 3 | 0 | 0 |
| City agencies | 8 | 2 | 2 |
| Food pantries | 2 | 0 | 0 |
| Vocational agencies | 2 | 0 | 0 |
| Miscellaneous | 4 | 0 | 0 |

[a]Includes agencies such as the Association for Retarded Citizens (ARC) and the United Cerebral Palsy (UCP) Association.

[b]Includes three homes for pregnant women.

cies received a second letter describing how they were to collect the data, the specific data to be collected, and other pertinent information. Twenty-two (63%) of the 35 participating agencies were able to identify one or more adult parents with mental retardation. These agencies then helped in collecting specific data on these parents and indicated which of them would be available to participate in Stage 2. Two methodological issues presented difficulties. Since for all participating agencies client contact was a confidential matter, a suitable way had to be devised whereby they could provide the needed information for the total count and maintain confidentiality, while still allowing the referred client to be identified by the referral source so that the latter could make initial contact when an interview was indicated. A method was devised that used client initials, number of client children, zip codes, whether the children were in or out of the home, and the agency's willingness to approach the client about participating in the study. The goal of this strategy was to keep duplication of probands to a minimum. In addition, this coding also rated the suitability of the client for further contact and interview.

The second methodological issue revolved around the criteria for mental retardation. Agencies that serve a range of clients other than the population targeted by this study often did not have access to psychometric testing data that would definitively categorize a parent, even though agency suspicion for such a case was strong. Agencies were supplied with a modified Einstein Parent Screening Instrument (Kaminer, Jedrysek, & Soles, 1981; Kaminer & Cohen, 1983) to be employed in the absence of a documented diagnosis of mental retardation (Figure 2.1). They were informed that as many of their referrals as possible would be tested in order to validate the classification.

## Stage 2: Identified Client

Stage 2 was instituted to validate referrals and to obtain interview data from the parents. Client participants were tested and interviewed at home or at the referring agency by a single interviewer with a master's degree in special education. A Slosson Intelligence Test-Revised (SIT-R) (Slosson, 1985) was administered to all adult participants along with the structured interview developed for the survey.

Forty-two of the parents were referred for, and completed this additional testing and interviewing. (The initial aim was to test a subset of 100 parents; these 42 represent all those parents for whom the caseworkers or other referring agency professionals cooperated in facilitating an interview appointment.)

## Results

Four hundred twenty-one clients were identified by the participating agencies. After cross-checking coded referrals, a total of 402 separate parents with mental retardation were identified, with only 19 (4.5%) clients having been referred by more than one agency. Of these 402 individuals, 30 were male, 280 were female, and 92 remain unidentified by sex (due to the use of initials and failure of the agency to specify sex). Information concerning children was available on 388 of the 402 referred parents. Of 1096 children identified, 601 (55%) were in the home and 495 (45%) were out of the home either because they had been removed by the authorities or were old enough to leave the home on their own. There was a mean of 2.83 children per parent with mental retardation. Information on the children of the other fourteen parents is unclear, with agency responses such as "three kids?" or "?." Three children born to this population and subsequently deceased were not included in the count. Two children in utero were counted as "in home."

1.  Inability to travel alone on public transportation; always comes to clinic accompanied by another adult

2.  Reading and writing problems seen when filling out applications:
    a.  Inability to write
    b.  Writing minimal factual information only
    c.  Reading words but limited comprehension

3.  Erratic appointment keeping (e.g., early, late, odd excuses, wrong day)

4.  Providing vague or naive information about basic facts (e.g., not certain what hospital the child was born in, not sure if child is on formula, not sure if child is in special education, unclear how to recognize fever)

5.  Problems managing money (e.g., trouble making change for dollar, out of money by second week of month when it seems it should last longer with some sort of budgeting, cannot estimate costs)

6.  Being overwhelmed by routine demands (e.g., appropriate dressing of child for weather, missing many appointments, no organization around house, inability to keep track of grocery needs, inability to sequence tasks or prioritize demands and activities)

7.  Child management difficulty of excessive degree observed or reported (e.g., lack of eye contact with child, fussing at child more than reinforcing appropriate behavior, inappropriate picking up of child, inappropriate feeding habits, child appearing to be in control of parent both behaviorally and intellectually)

8.  Using covering-up techniques to conceal deficit (e.g., "He's going to get that toy for Christmas;" "We had a thermometer until last week")

9.  Central role of "benefactor"; requires help not expected for an adult (e.g., help with filling out forms, transportation, getting groceries, calling to schedule doctors appointments)

10. Historical information documenting impairment/mental retardation from:
    a.  Self-report (e.g., "I was in a special education class for being slow.")
    b.  Family member (e.g., "Sure she graduated; a special school district gave her a diploma.")
    c.  Social agency

If all 10 difficulties are occurring or five of the first nine are occurring, this adult should be considered a candidate for testing to determine if he or she has mental retardation.

Figure 2.1.   Checklist for identification of intellectual impairment in parents. (Adapted from the Einstein Parent Screening Instrument, Kaminer, 1983.)

Of those 42 parents who completed Stage 2 testing and interview, 37 tested in the range of mental retardation with an SIT-R intelligence quotient (IQ) of 69 or below. The other five tested between 71 and 79. An examination of these five protocols indicates prominent scatter and suggests that all five of these adults may have had an overlapping learning disability or language disorder resulting in an overall functional level in the range of mild mental retardation. They were excluded from the data on mental retardation for clarity in the sample. The average SIT-R IQ of those 37 who tested as having mental retardation was 52 (range 35–69). These 37 individuals included two males and 35 females. The average SIT-R IQ of the five individuals who did not have mental retardation was 74. The 37 parents with mental retardation represented 105 children, 78 at home and 27 removed from home. Those children at home had an average age of 4.5 years (range 5 weeks to 12 years). There was no way to determine the age of those children who had been removed. Twenty-five of these parents were single, 9 were married, and 3 were separated from their spouses (Table 2.5).

In addition to testing and interviewing the parents, an attempt was made to test at least one preschool child in every family. In most cases, this child was selected on the basis of the parental response to the question, "Which child are you most worried about?". This testing was performed at the time of the parent interview. SIT-R IQ scores were obtained on 25 children representing 25 parents. The mean SIT-R IQ score for the 25 children tested was 73 (range 36–117). The IQ levels of the children showed no correlation with the IQ levels of the parents ($r = 0.05$). Table 2.6 shows these children's IQ scores in relation to those of their parents.

The interview conducted with all 37 parents with mental retardation investigated their strengths, weaknesses, and struggles with parenting (Table 2.7). A significant number of problems emerged. More than two thirds of these parents perceived that their children had learning, behavioral, and medical problems. Only 15% of the parents reported any previous input (e.g., from school or social service agencies) with regard to parenting and childrearing skills. More than half of these parents were aware of having been reported for child abuse/neglect in the past. Although 93% reported some satisfaction with being a parent, 71% emphatically stated that they could not handle any more children.

Table 2.5.    Characteristics of 37 parents with mental retardation

|  | Mean | Range |
|---|---|---|
| Age | 29 | 17–48 |
| Number of children | 3 | 1–8 |
| Number of children in home | 2 | 1–5 |
| SIT-R IQ | 52 | 35–69 |
| Basal mental age | 7 years 10 months | 3 years 11 months– 9 years 4 months |
| Highest item passes | 8 years 8 months | 5 years 9 months– 12 years 1 month |

| Classification | N | Percent |
|---|---|---|
| Mild mental retardation | 14 | 38 |
| Moderate mental retardation | 20 | 54 |
| Severe mental retardation | 3 | 8 |
| Total | 37 | 100 |

## STUDY TWO: ST. LOUIS COUNTY

The second survey was conducted in St. Louis county in 1985–1986. The design was relatively unchanged from Study 1 with the exception that the key informant was asked to complete an additional questionnaire regarding his or her view of client needs.

### Stage 1: Key Informant

Of the 128 agencies contacted, 72 (57%) agreed to participate. The remaining 56 (44%) declined participation. Of the 72 participating agencies, 33 had no way to identify any persons in their client population who met the criteria of the study; therefore, they declined participation at second contact, leaving a total of 36 participating agencies. A total of 84 parents with mental retardation were identified by the remaining 32 agencies. Cross-checking to eliminate duplicates left a total of 73 separate parents with mental retardation (64 female and 9 male). Ages were supplied for only 23 of these parents. Of this subsample, the average age was 31.6 years with a range of 16–50 years of age. There were five married couples in the population of 73 parents, for a total of 68 families. These 68 families represented 151 children, 102 reported to be in the home and 38 out of the home. The status of 16 children remains unclear. Two children in utero were counted as "in home." Using a base

Table 2.6. IQ characteristics of the children of 25 parents with mental retardation

| Parent IQ mean (range) (AAMR classification) | Parent age mean (range) | Child IQ (classification) | Number of children | Child age mean (range) |
|---|---|---|---|---|
| Mild mental retardation (N = 7) 65 (56–65) | 33 (17–48) | Normal (85) | 5 | 4.5 (3.3– 6.7) |
| | | Slow learner (70–84) | 1 | |
| | | Mental retardation (69) | 1 | |
| Moderate mental retardation (N = 15) 44.5 (42–50) | 26 16–40 | Normal | 5 | 4.8 (0.7– 17.0) |
| | | Slow learner | 2 | |
| | | Mild mental retardation | 1 | |
| | | Moderate mental retardation | 4 | |
| | | Severe mental retardation | 3 | |
| Severe mental retardation (N = 3) 37.5 (35–39) | 32 (27–42) | Normal | 2 | 4.8 (0.3– 11.4) |
| | | Mild mental retardation | 1 | |

Table 2.7.   Problems, resources, and supports relevant to parents with mental retardation

| Problems with children | Number ($N = 37$) | | | Percent | |
|---|---|---|---|---|---|
| Medical | 24 | | | 65 | |
| Behavioral | 23 | | | 62 | |
| Learning | 24 | | | 65 | |

| Parental resources | Yes | | No | | Does not know | |
|---|---|---|---|---|---|---|
| | $N$ | Percent | $N$ | Percent | $N$ | Percent |
| Previous classes in child-rearing | 4 | 11 | 33 | 89 | | |
| Known child abuse hotline calls | 20 | 54 | 17 | 46 | | |
| Do you like being a parent | 35 | 95 | 2 | 5 | | |
| Do you plan more children | 7[a] | 19 | 25 | 68 | 5 | 13 |
| Are you able to have more children | 19 | 51 | 15 | 41 | 3 | 8 |

| Environmental supports | | | |
|---|---|---|---|
| Income | | $N$ | Percent |
| Supplemental Security Income (SSI) (for self or other) | | 18 | 49 |
| Aid to Dependent Children | | 19 | 51 |
| Food stamps | | 7 | 19 |
| Interviewee employed | | 2 | 5 |
| Spouse employed | | 4 | 11 |
| Extended family support | | 4 | 11 |
| None | | 2 | 5 |
| Refusal to reveal | | 1 | 3 |
| Family support: emotional | | | |
| Yes | | 19 | 51 |
| No | | 8 | 22 |
| Sometimes | | 10 | 27 |
| Source of family help | | | |
| Mother of client | | 21 | 57 |
| Father of client | | 7 | 19 |
| Sibling(s) of client | | 16 | 43 |
| In-laws | | 3 | 8 |
| Grandparents of client | | 2 | 5 |
| Aunts or uncles of client | | 5 | 14 |
| Cousin | | 1 | 3 |
| Shunted around family | | 2 | 5 |

[a]One parent stated that she planned more children, then replied that she was unable to have more.

of 68 families, the average number of children per family was 2.2 with a range from 1 to 7 (Figure 2.2).

## Stage 2: Identified Client

A 10% subset of these parents completed testing and interviewing. As with Study 1, the aim of this subset was to validate the referral base and to discover from the parents their needs. These eight parents (all mothers) represent 23 children.

## Results

SIT-R testing of these eight mothers validated all as having mental retardation (average IQ 61, range 43–69). Five of these eight mothers allowed testing of one of their preschool children. The children's IQ's were 100, 104, 80, 65, 62. All but one of these mothers reported significant behavioral and disciplinary problems with their children. Parenting techniques described by these mothers ranged from begging the children to behave to excessive spanking. Referral sources documented a number of children with developmental delays, parenting problems including lack of nurturing and lack of discipline, emotional difficulties in the children, other neurodevelopmental problems, and one case of Tourette syndrome.

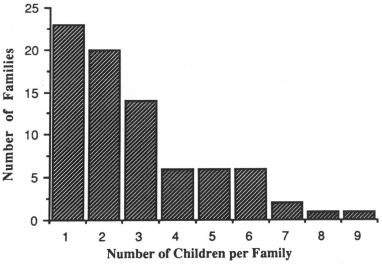

Figure 2.2.   Distribution of family size in secondary survey (St. Louis county).

## Client Needs as Perceived by the Key Informant

As noted, all key informants were asked to complete a questionnaire to determine the needs of parents with mental retardation from the perspective of those service providers who attempt to work with this population. The questionnaire was completed by 15 agencies and by 17 Division of Family Service (DFS) Social Service Workers (total $n = 32$). Four questions highlighted the key informant views of the needs of the clients in general and the specific issues of service needs (Figures 2.3, 2.4, 2.5, 2.6).

Not unexpectedly, a lack of parenting skills emerges as the primary perceived problem for these adults (Figure 2.3). However, of equal concern, at least in the eyes of these service providers, is the inability of these parents to utilize the social, health, and welfare service systems, thus compounding the problems by excluding remediation/support efforts (Figure 2.4). The service providers identified a number of services necessary to enable these parents to function more effectively. Foremost among these were transportation to and from services, housing, parent education, money management, day and respite care services, family life education and counseling. Somewhat realistically, job training for most of these parents took a back seat to these service needs. When caseworkers were

---

In your opinion, which of the following areas reflect the five (5) most serious problems faced by parents with developmental disabilities?

|  | N | Percent |
|---|---|---|
| Inadequate parenting skills | 26 | 81 |
| Poverty | 17 | 53 |
| Lack of adequate housing | 15 | 47 |
| Lack of daily living skills | 14 | 44 |
| Child neglect | 12 | 38 |
| Transportation | 11 | 34 |
| Family conflict | 11 | 34 |
| Lack of vocational skills | 10 | 31 |
| Lack of adequate medical/health care | 10 | 31 |
| Lack of basic social skills | 9 | 28 |
| Lack of communication skills | 6 | 19 |
| Child abuse | 5 | 16 |

Figure 2.3.  Key Informant Questionnaire Responses I.

What factors, if any, do you feel would keep adults with developmental disabilities from seeking help from existing service agencies?

| | N | Percent |
|---|---|---|
| Lack of knowledge of services available | 30 | 94 |
| Lack of knowledge of how to apply for services | 29 | 91 |
| Transportation | 29 | 91 |
| Lack of necessary skills in locating agency site | 26 | 81 |
| Cost of service | 18 | 56 |
| Service location | 15 | 47 |
| Insensitivity of service personnel to the special needs of the applicant | 7 | 22 |
| Embarrassment about what others might think | 6 | 19 |
| Inability to use telephone | 3 | 9 |
| Agency usually not open when help is needed | 3 | 9 |
| Other | | |
|    Lack of motivation to apply | 4 | 13 |
|    Inability to recognize need for help | 3 | 9 |

Figure 2.4.   Key Informant Questionnaire Responses II.

asked to identify their most difficult problems with these parents, poor judgment was most frequently mentioned. Many other problems that reflect this poor judgment were also listed, for example, inability to manage money, birth control and sexuality, and unrealistic expectations for their children. Another significant problem noted was the lack of extended family support. Other difficulties became even more problematic when there was no family support to "run interference," as it were, between the adult with mental retardation and the rest of the world.

## DISCUSSION AND CONCLUSIONS

Conducting this kind of survey is extremely difficult for two reasons: First, the population of parents who have mental retardation tends to be highly mobile, and second, their difficulties with telling time leads to a high rate of failure to keep appointments. In addition, the use of an IQ test, whether a screening instrument or a full psychometric battery, raises methodological concerns. Criteria for the diagnosis of mental

Please indicate from the following list the services you believe are needed to address the problem areas you encounter most often in serving parents with developmental disabilities.

| | N | Percent |
|---|---|---|
| Transportation to and from services | 25 | 78 |
| Housing | 23 | 72 |
| Parent education services | 22 | 69 |
| Money management | 22 | 69 |
| Day care for children | 21 | 66 |
| Family life education | 19 | 59 |
| Counseling | 19 | 59 |
| Respite services for children | 17 | 53 |
| Job skills training | 17 | 53 |
| Parent to parent networking and support | 16 | 50 |
| Recreation/leisure | 16 | 50 |
| Respite services for parents | 14 | 44 |
| Sheltered workshop | 14 | 44 |
| Adult day services | 13 | 41 |
| Other | | |
| Homemaker | 2 | |

Figure 2.5.    Key Informant Questionnaire Responses III.

What difficulties do you encounter most frequently in providing services for parents with developmental disabilities?

> Poor judgment
> Lack of ability to budget
> Lack of money
> Being easily exploited
> Birth control and sexuality
> Extended family not supportive
> Lack of parenting skills
> Unrealistic expectations for children
> Lack of stimulation of children

Figure 2.6.    Key Informant Questionnaire Responses IV.

retardation include social impairments and onset during the developmental period, in addition to a significantly depressed IQ level. An adult with severe cognitive limitations may function similarly to an adult with mental retardation but may have reached that behavioral limit as a result of many different factors. The psychological assessment of a child always attempts to take into account such complicating events as chronic physical illness, emotional disorder in the child, psychiatric disorder in the family, deprivation, poor nutrition, and educational neglect, for interpretation of IQ scores. An adult with cognitive limitations who was never adequately assessed in childhood or whose records are for various reasons unavailable can present a difficult diagnostic dilemma in which the use and interpretation of any screening IQ instrument can be questioned. Retrospectively, we realize that, although it would still not respond to all possible objections, the use of an instrument such as the Vineland Adaptive Behavior Scales (Sparrow, Balla, & Cicchetti, 1984a; Sparrow, Balla, & Cicchetti, 1984b) would probably be more sensitive than an IQ test in an adult population.

Despite these limitations, and taking all biases into account, the data indicate that in the community there are a significant number of adults with mental retardation who are parents. The overwhelming majority of these parents report significant problems with their children, with their parenting role, and in their role as income providers. Almost none have been prepared in any way for any of these roles. Further, there are few, if any, resources to support them in this effort. Many of these parents are remanded to protective services, which tends to be more punitive than supportive.

Nonetheless, the data also reflect that the professionals who work with these parents can identify their limitations with sensitivity, leading to few false positives. (The false negative rate remains unknown.)

The parents with mental retardation identified in this study tended to have between two and three children. They did not exhibit the differential fertility rate that assigns a lower reproductive rate to parents with the more severe degrees of mental retardation. If this differential fertility rate does apply, it may only reach significance with parents who have severe to profound levels of mental retardation. Social isolation and restricted opportunity may have contributed to its validity in the past.

In terms of calculating a reproductive rate based on population figures, the data will not support strong conclusions. In general it appears that parents with mental retardation are having slightly more children than the general population. However, the fraction of women with mental retardation having children appears to be one third the rate of the general population of women.

The IQ levels of the children showed no correlation with the IQ levels of the parents (see Table 2.6). In contrast to Reed and Reed (1965), only 12 of the 31 children tested were functioning in the range of mental retardation, and, in most cases, a significant part of the retardation could be attributed to the level and lack of appropriateness of the environmental stimulation.

The low percentage of duplicated referrals (4.5% city and 13.1% county) suggests that many parents who have mental retardation are not known to more than one service agency. By extension, many such parents may not be known to any agency. Only 40 (10.0%) city and 13 (17.8%) county agencies identified parents with mental retardation as known to the Regional Center's caseload as receiving services. This suggests that networking in order to provide service for these clients has not yet developed to an optimal level, so that many of these parents are falling through the service net.

Further complicating the lack of services is a failure or reluctance to identify these adults as having mental retardation. Possibly two to three times more parents with mental retardation could have been identified. Noting that only 50% of the agencies who might work with this population responded, an underestimate could result. However, the fact that many parents with mental retardation were identified by only one agency further suggests that many of these clients are not coming to agency attention, and that those who are coming to attention are not being identified as needing extra services.

The zip code identification of clients was used to locate parents with mental retardation and their children in both the city and county. Zip code mapping paralleled the distribution of low-income families in the greater St. Louis area. Thus, these parents and their children are living in low-income, high-risk (e.g., lead paint, crime, shysters) environments with little knowledge of how to seek and/or use services and, even when services would be sought, no transportation to get there. Thus their children are at a multiplicative risk from poverty, unsafe environments, and parents with cognitive impairment.

The significant number of these parents whose children had been removed from their care (greater than 25%) documents an unmet need for parent training and other supportive services that can capitalize on these parents' good intentions, remediate their shortcomings, and recognize and support their positive assets. Clearly, the parents and their children are "hidden" and at high risk. A maximum effort to identify these families and channel them to appropriate services is necessary if we are to prevent a "cycle of retardedness" that parallels the "cycle of poverty."

## REFERENCES

Kaminer, R., Jedrysek, E., & Soles, B. (1981). Intellectually limited parents. *Journal of Developmental and Behavioral Pediatrics, 2,* 39–43.

Kaminer, R., & Cohen, H. (1983). Intellectually limited mothers. In *Developmental handicaps, prevention and treatment* (pp. 24–44). Washington, DC: American Association of University Affiliated Programs for Persons with Developmental Disabilities.

Klerman, G.L. (1986). The National Institute of Mental Health-Epidemiologic Catchment Area (NIMH-ECA) Program: Background, preliminary findings and implications. *Social Psychiatry, 21,* 159–166.

Reed, E.W., & Reed, S.C. (1965). *Mental retardation: A family study.* Philadelphia: W.B. Saunders.

Slosson, K. (1985). *The Slosson Intelligence Test for Children and Adults.* East Aurora, New York: Slosson Educational Publications.

Sparrow, S. S., Balla, D. A., & Cicchetti, D. V. (1984a). *Vineland Adaptive Behavior Scales: Interview edition: Expanded form manual.* Circle Pines, MN: American Guidance Service.

Sparrow, S. S., Balla, D. A., & Cicchetti, D. V. (1984b). *Vineland Adaptive Behavior Scales: Interior edition: Survey form manual.* Circle Pines, MN: American Guidance Service.

Tremblay, M.-A. (1957). The key informant technique: A non-ethnographic application. *American Anthropologist, 59,* 688–698.

Warheit, G., Buhl, J., Bell, R. (1978). A critique of social indicators analysis and key informants surveys as needs assessment methods. *Education and Program Planning, 1,* 239–247.

Whitman, B., Graves, B., & Accardo, P. (1987). Mentally retarded parents in the community: Identification method and needs assessment survey. *American Journal of Mental Deficiency 91,* (6), 636–638.

# 3 || Genetics and Mental Retardation

## Noreen D'Souza

During the 1960s throughout the 1980s, there have been striking advances in genetics. The concurrent development of clinical cytogenetics and clinical genetic services has had significant impact in deliverance of medical care to persons with mental retardation, particularly in terms of genetic diagnostic evaluation and more accurate genetic counseling. Today, genetic services are a routine component in the care of a child with mental retardation. Genetic counseling services are also being increasingly utilized by unaffected family members when faced with the occurrence of mental retardation in their family.

It is also being realized that attention should be given to the needs of adults/parents with mental retardation for clinical genetic services. There are two main factors that have contributed to the recognition of this need. First is the increased longevity of individuals who have mental retardation and survival into adulthood (Baird & Sadovnick, 1987; Emery & Rimoin, 1983). The second was discovered from several epidemiological

Table 3.1.   AAMD (1977) and ICD-9 (1980) definitions of levels of mental retardation according to IQ

| Level of mental retardation | AAMD | ICD-9 |
| --- | --- | --- |
| Mild | 55–69 | 50–70 |
| Moderate | 40–54 | 35–69 |
| Severe | 25–39 | 20–34 |
| Profound | 24 | 20 |

studies that recognize different levels of mental retardation (McLaren & Bryson, 1987).

The AAMD defines mental retardation as "significantly subaverage general intellectual function existing concurrently with deficits in adaptive behavior, and manifested during the developmental period" (Grossman, 1973). Thus, by this definition, there should be both significantly subaverage intellectual function and deficits in adaptive behavior to designate an individual as having mental retardation. However, in common practice, the designation is made based on IQ scores. Table 3.1 shows the various levels (based on IQ scores) according to the American Association on Mental Deficiency (AAMD) (Grossman, 1977) and ICD-9 (Internation Classification of Diseases) definitions (World Health Organization, 1980). If a person has an IQ higher than 69 or 70, he or she is not designated as having mental retardation. IQ levels between 50 and 70 are considered as representing mild mental retardation. Individuals above the mild level, but under an IQ of 80, are classified as having borderline intelligence. The great majority of persons with mental retardation fall into the mild category, live at home or in the community and are partially self-sufficient (Berini & Kahn, 1987). Though the etiology is not clear in a large number of these cases, genetic factors are felt to play a significant role. In severe mental retardation, which makes up approximately 10% of persons with mental retardation, genetic disorders are thought to account for approximately one third of the instances (Emery & Rimoin, 1983). Some of these disorders can be identified in the presymptomatic stage and treated successfully.

## ETIOLOGY OF MENTAL RETARDATION

Though the etiology is unknown in the majority of instances and, in some instances, remains inferred, a consideration of all etiologic factors is essential in establishing a diagnosis. Recently identified causative factors such as fragile X can be tested for using newer cytogenetic and molecular genetic technologies (Opitz, Neri, Reynolds, & Spano, 1988). Similarly, DNA technologies can also be used in family studies for diagnosis of other single-gene disorders, such as phenylketonuria (PKU) (Woo, Lidsky, & Guttler, 1988), tuberous sclerosis (Fryer et al., 1987), and neurofibromatosis (Barker, Wright, & Nguyen, 1987).

Etiologic factors include the full spectrum of purely nongenetic and purely genetic conditions, as well as disorders involving both genetic and environmental components. The various factors can also be considered from the standpoint of prenatal, perinatal, or postnatal (McLaren & Bryson, 1987). Table 3.2 shows an etiologic classification of mental retardation (Berini & Kahn, 1987). Table 3.3 (McLaren & Bryson, 1987) shows the contribution of these various etiologies in both severe and mild mental retardation.

## GENETIC FORMS OF MENTAL RETARDATION: CLASSIFICATION AND MODES OF INHERITANCE

There is a wide spectrum of genetic disorders with varying modes of inheritance. Table 3.4 shows a classification that applies to genetic disorders in general.

### Chromosomal Abnormalities

Chromosome abnormalities have been found to be a significant causal factor in mental retardation. Several studies have been done looking at chromosome abnormalities in mild mental retardation (scores of IQ 50–70) and severe mental retardation (all instances of mental retardation with IQ below 50). In the latter group, chromosomal etiologies in the various studies accounted for almost one quarter of the instances and ranged from a low of about 20% to a high of almost 40% (Fryers & McKay, 1979; McDonald, 1973). These differences in rates could be related to the method of ascertainment in that some investigators with higher estimates have included nonsurvivors. In mild mental retardation, fewer chromosome abnormalities have been found and ranged from 4.3 to 7.8% (McLaren & Bryson, 1987).

Trisomy 21, or Down syndrome, has been the most com-

Table 3.2.    Common causes of mental retardation

**Genetic**

Chromosomal disorders
Inborn errors of metabolism
Hereditary degenerative disorders
Hormonal deficiencies
Primary CNS defects
Malformation syndromes
Sporadic syndromes with unidentified etiology, possibly genetic
Familial idiopathic mental retardation
Low end of normal distribution

**Acquired**

*Prenatal*

Infection (e.g., syphilis, rubella, toxoplasmosis, cytomegalic inclusion disease)
Fetal irradiation
Toxins (e.g., fetal alcohol syndrome, lead poisoning, mercury poisoning, fetal hydantoin syndrome)
Maternal metabolic problems (e.g., maternal PKU)

*Perinatal*

Prematurity
Asphyxia (e.g., abruptio placentai, cord prolapse, meconium aspiration)
Infection (e.g., meningitis, encephalitis, TORCH [toxoplasmosis, rubella, cytomegalovirus, herpes] agents, syphilis, herpes simplex)
Trauma (e.g., breech delivery, intracerebral hemorrhage)
Hypoglycemia
Kernicterus

*Postnatal*

Brain injury (e.g., trauma, drowning, lightning)
Poisoning (e.g., lead, carbon monoxide)
Cerebrovascular accidents
Postimmunization encephalopathy (e.g., pertussis, rabies)
Infection (meningitis, encephalitis, abscess)
Early severe malnutrition
Hormonal deficiency
Psychosocial deprivation, abuse, or neglect

Adapted from Berini, R. and Kahn, E. (1987).

Table 3.3. Etiology of mental retardation[b]

| Study | Subject population (n) | Method of ascertainment (date) | Prenatal | | | | Perinatal | | | Postnatal | | Unknown |
|---|---|---|---|---|---|---|---|---|---|---|---|---|
| | | | Chromosomal | Single gene | Multifactorial | Environmental | Infections or other | Hypoxia | Premature or low birthweight | Trauma or neglect | Disease or other | |
| **Severe** | | | | | | | | | | | | |
| McQueen et al., 1986 (Maritime Provinces) | 7–10-year-olds; IQ < 55 (n = 196) | Multiple identifying agencies (1980) | 24.5[a] | 4.6 | 16.8 | 11.2 | 3.5 | 6.6 | | | 3.6 | 29 |
| Einfeld, 1984 (Sydney, Australia) | 0–20-year-olds; IQ < 50 (n = 3,208) | Assessment clinic (1970–1982) | 23.5 | 3.2 | 22.4 | ←8.5→ | | | 3.4 | 11 | 2.8 | 24.4 |
| Willard et al., 1982 (France) | 3–17-year-olds; institutionalized IQ < 50 (n = 124) | 3 institutions (1981) | 21 | 3.2 | 10 | 5.6 | | 25 | | 0.8 | 2.8 | 33 |
| Elwood and Darragh, 1981 (Northern Ireland) | Born 1955–1976; IQ < 50 (n = 1,777) | Registered mentally retarded (1980) | 38 | 5 | | 1 | 2.5 | 3.7 | 5.1 | 0.6 | 2.8 | 40 |
| Hunter et al., 1980 (Manitoba) | 20-year-olds; institutionalized before 1977; IQ < 50 (n = 406) | Institutions (1975–1978) | 13.5 | 12.5 | 1.7 | 4.9 | 5.6 | 4.2 | 3.2 | 3.7 | 8.8 | 41.9 |
| Fryers and MacKay, 1979 (Salford, England) | Registered 1961–1977; IQ < 50 (n = 401) | Multiple agencies (1978) | 18.9 | | 41 | 1.2 | ←12.2→ | | | 4.5 | 6.7 | 14.8 |
| Gustavson et al., 1977 (Sweden) | Born 1959–1970; alive at 1 year; IQ < 50 (n = 161) | Registered mentally retarded (1975–1976) | 36 | 7 | ←10→ | | 2 | 8 | | | 3 | 34 |
| Gustavson et al., 1977 (Sweden) | Born 1959–1970; alive at 1 year; IQ < 50 (n = 161) | Board of services for mentally retarded persons (1975–1976) | 34.8 | | 24.9 | 8.1 | none | 7.5 | 0.6 | | 1.2 | 22.9 |
| Laxova et al., 1977 (Hertfordshire, England) | Born 1965–1968; alive 1972; IQ < 50 (n = 146) | Multiple agencies (1974) | 32.9 | 14.4 | 11.7 | 0.7 | | 0.7 | | 0.7 | 2.1 | 36.9 |
| McDonald, 1973 (Quebec) | Born in 1958; IQ < 50 (n = 507) | Multiple identifying agencies (1966–1969) | 23 | 21 | | | 7–11 | | 3 | 1 | 8 to 11 | 30 to 37 |
| **Mild** | | | | | | | | | | | | |
| Einfeld, 1984 (Sydney, Australia) | 0–20-year-olds; IQ = 52–67 (n = 344) | Assessment clinic (1970–1982) | 7.8 | | 16.6 | ←3.9→ | | | 4.3 | 14.7 | 3.4 | 49 |
| Hagberg et al., 1981 (city of Gothenburg, Sweden) | Born 1966–1970; IQ = 50–70 (n = 91) | Multiple agencies (1978–1979) | 4.3 | 1 | 11 | 8.8 | 1 | 18.6 | | ←2→ | | 62.6 |
| Son Blomquist et al., 1981 (Northern Sweden) | Born 1959–1970; IQ = 50–69 (n = 171) | Registered with board for services for mentally retarded persons (1975–1979) | 7.6 | 8.2 | 23.4 | 8.2 | 1.2 | 5.3 | 0.6 | 2.3 | 2.3 | 45 |

[a] Percentage of mentally retarded population studied.  [b] From McLaren & Bryson, 1987, p. 250; reprinted with permission.

Table 3.4.    Classification of
genetic disorders

Chromosome abnormalities
Single-gene defects
    Autosomal dominant
    Autosomal recessive
    X-linked
Multifactorial disorders
Congenital malformations
Teratogenic syndromes

mon chromosomal abnormality reported in individuals with mental retardation (Emery & Rimoin, 1983). IQ scores vary widely. Though the IQ range is generally said to be 25–75, the mean IQ for older patients is 24. Mosaics (mixture of normal cells and Trisomy 21 cells) can fall into the mild retardation groups. Increased incidence of Trisomy 21 has been found with advancing maternal age. The great majority of cases (94%) are due to nondisjunction in meiosis. The remainder result from translocation (3.3%) and mosaicism (2.4%). Risk of recurrence in the nondisjunction instances is approximately 1–2%. Translocation type may be either de novo or result from a balanced translocation carrier status in a parent. Risk of recurrence in the former case is approximately 1–2%. In the latter case, it depends on which parent is a carrier. A female translocation carrier has a risk of approximately 8–15% and a male carrier a risk of less than 5% in future offspring. Adult females with Down syndrome can reproduce and theoretically have a 50% chance of having an offspring with Down syndrome (De-Grouchy & Turleau, 1984). No cases of paternity have been reported. Males with Down syndrome have relatively low serum testosterone values and are considered infertile (Smith, 1988).

*Other Autosomal Trisomies*    Trisomy 18 and 13 are both associated with severe mental retardation. However, they have a poor prognosis and the majority of persons affected do not survive beyond early childhood. In instances of persons with mosaics of these trisomies, there is a better prognosis and survival may go into adulthood. Also, such persons are likely to have less severe mental retardation. Trisomy 8 usually occurs in a mosaic situation. In most such instances, mental retardation is in the mild to moderate range. IQ varies between 12 and 94, with an average of between 45 and 75 (DeGrouchy & Turleau, 1984). In one third of instances, the diagnosis was performed in adulthood. In general, affected persons are calm, even tempered, and sociable, but occasionally anxiety-ridden, or given to bouts with anger. They have language difficulties. Seizures have been reported (Smith, 1988).

*Partial Deletions and Duplications*   These abnormalities have been reported in almost every chromosome. Most of these conditions are associated with mental retardation. Also, with the advent of high resolution banding, small chromosomal deletions have been found in some malformation syndromes, for example, an interstitial deletion is seen in the number 15 chromosome at the q11−13 region in at least 50% of instances of Prader-Willi syndrome (Niikawa & Ishikiriyama, 1985). This syndrome is characterized by mental limitation, hypotonia, obesity, and small hands and feet. IQ ranges from 20 to 80, most commonly being 40−60.

*Sex Chromosomal Abnormalities*   In general, sex chromosomal abnormalities are felt to be less likely to be associated with mental retardation. However, the discovery by Lubs of a fragile site on the long arm of the X chromosome in affected males and some carrier females led to the recognition of the fragile X syndrome (Lubs, 1969). This condition is fairly common and has an estimated incidence of approximately 1 in 2000 males and 1 in 2500 females (Turner & Jacobs, 1983). In males, the syndrome is characterized by mental retardation, large ears, and macro-orchidism. Average intelligence is in the range of moderate mental retardation, though affected individuals present with mild or severe mental retardation. Speech development is disproportionately delayed. Other features include hyperextensible joints, and autistic behaviours such as hand flapping, hand biting, eye avoidance, and perseverative speech. In a cytogenetic study of autistic individuals, approximately 5% were found to be fragile X positive (Watson, Leckman, Annex, Breg, & Boles, 1984). Furthermore, the fragile X has also been found in boys with learning disabilities and attentional problems whose IQ extended into the normal range (Hagerman, Randi, Kemper, & Hudson, 1985). Heterozygous females may have no mental disability or may show mild mental retardation in about one third of instances. Screening mentally retarded individuals for fragile X cytogenetically will identify all males who are positive for fragile X except the 1−2% functioning within the low-normal range of intelligence (Turner, Robinson, Long, & Purvis-Smith, 1986). Of the females, 90% of those expressing the heterozygous state will be positive for fragile X. A further group of carrier females can be identified among female relatives of probands. However, only 25% of the heterozygotes with normal intelligence will be positive for fragile X (Sherman, Morton, Jacobs, & Turner, 1984).

Although the fragile X syndrome is an X-linked form of mental retardation, it does not follow dominant or recessive patterns. Women who carry the gene have a 50% chance of transmitting it to each son or daughter. However, it appears that 20% of males who have the gene do not have mental retardation.

Other sex chromosome abnormalities, such as the Klinefelter variants—XXXY and XXXXY syndrome—are associated with mental retardation. IQ's range from 19 to 57 with a mean of 34. In the classical Klinefelter syndrome, that is, patients with XXY karyotype, affected boys tend to be normal in performance IQ but less so in verbal IQ. They are described as having a "dull" mentality. About 15–20% of affected persons have an IQ below 80. They have a high incidence of behavioral problems. Mental retardation is also seen in the Quadruple X (XXXX) syndrome and Penta X syndrome. These conditions are relatively uncommon.

## SINGLE GENE DEFECTS

Currently there are more than 4500 genetic disorders listed in McKusick's catalogue, *Mendelian Inheritance in Man* (1988). The three main categories are autosomal dominant, autosomal recessive and X-linked. Common examples from each category are briefly discussed here with risks of recurrence.

### Autosomal Dominant (AD)

Where autosomal dominance exists, the disorder is manifest in the heterozygote state which can be denoted as Aa, where A represents the normal gene and a represents an abnormal gene. The main characteristics are as follows (Thompson & Thompson, 1986):

1. The trait appears in every generation, exhibiting vertical transmission.
2. Any child of an affected person has a 50% risk of inheriting the trait.

3. Unaffected family members do not transmit the trait to their children.
4. The occurrence and transmission of the trait are not influenced by sex. Other features that have a bearing on the clinical features of AD disorders are the concepts of incomplete penetrance and variable expressivity.

*Penetrance*   Applies to the likelihood of a gene being expressed at all. When some individuals who have the appropriate genotype fail to express it, the trait is said to exhibit reduced penetrance. Expressivity refers to the degree of expression, that is, whether clinically the condition is expressed in a mild, moderate, or severe form. Below are commonly occurring examples of AD disorders associated with mental retardation.

*1.  Neurofibromatosis (NF)*   Neurofibromatosis has an estimated incidence of 1 in 3000 individuals. The disorder is characterized by multiple hyperpigmented spots ("cafe-au-lait" spots), and neurofibromas, which usually develop by early adulthood. The gene is highly penetrant, but shows wide variability in expression. According to Ricardi (1981), intellectual disability in one form or another involves at least 40% of patients with NF. Frank mental retardation accounts for perhaps 2–5% of persons with the disease. The gene has been localized to chromosome No. 17 (Barker, Wright, & Nguyen, 1987). DNA studies in family members can help to identify presymptomatic or asymptomatic individuals who carry the gene.

*2.  Tuberous Sclerosis*   Tuberous sclerosis is characterized by hamartomatous skin nodules, seizures, phakomata, and bone lesions. About 0.5% of individuals with severe mental retardation have this condition (Smith, 1988). There is wide variability in expression of the disease. Not all patients with skin lesions develop seizures, mental disability, or both. One general survey showed a 69% incidence of mental disability. The gene has been localized to chromosome No. 9, and DNA studies are helpful in some families to identify individuals who carry the gene (Fryer, 1987).

## Autosomal Recessive (AR)

Autosomal recessive conditions are manifested in the homozygous state, which can be denoted as aa, with a representing the disease gene, and AA denoting a normal genotype, with A representing the normal gene. Parents of an affected individual are carriers with a genotype of Aa and are generally themselves unaffected. Characteristics of autosomal recessive inheritance are as follows (Thompson & Thompson, 1986):

1. The trait characteristically appears only in sibs, not in their parents, offspring, or other relatives.
2. On the average, one fourth of the sibs of the proband are affected; in other words, the recurrence risk is one in four for each birth.
3. The parents of the affected child may be consanguinous.
4. Males and females are equally likely to be affected.

Examples of AR disorders associated with mental retardation include metabolic disorders, such as phenylketonuria and galactosemia. Mental retardation in these two conditions can be prevented by treatment. Adult females with PKU need to be treated during pregnancy, as elevated maternal phenylalanine levels have teratogenic effects on the fetus and can cause mental retardation in offspring. (Turner & Jacobs, 1983).

### X-Linked Disorders

In X-linked disorders, the abnormal gene is located on the X chromosome. Characteristics of X-linked recessive inheritance are as follows (Thompson & Thompson, 1986):

1. The incidence of the trait is much higher in males than in females.
2. The trait is passed from an affected man through all his daughters to, on the average, one half their sons.
3. The trait is never transmitted directly from father to son.
4. The trait may be transmitted through a series of carrier females; if so, the affected males in a kindred are related to one another through females.
5. Carriers show variable expression of the trait.

Examples include Lesch-Nyhan syndrome, which is characterized by mental retardation, choreoathetosis, self-mutilation, and hyperuricemia.

### MULTIFACTORIAL DISORDERS

Multifactorial disorders are determined by a combination of factors, genetic and possibly also nongenetic, each with only a minor effect. The term polygenic is often used interchangeably with the term multifactorial. These disorders tend to cluster in families but do not show any particular genetic pattern as seen with the single-gene traits. A large number of common conditions fall into this category. Examples include spina bifida and idiopathic seizures. It is felt that a significant percentage of cases of mental retardation of unknown etiology fall into this category.

## CONGENITAL MALFORMATIONS

Congenital malformations may be divided into two groups: 1) single central nervous system (CNS) malformation and 2) multiple congenital anomalies (MCA)/Mental Retardation (MR) (Opitz, 1980). Primary CNS malformations may be divided into several groups and are shown in Table 3.5. MCA/MR syndromes include many different syndromes having different modes of inheritance. Selected examples are presented in Table 3.6.

## TERATOGENIC SYNDROMES

Teratogenic syndromes are caused by in utero exposure to a specific agent and are not genetic. Common examples are fetal

Table 3.5.    Primary CNS malformation

| Disorder | Etiology |
| --- | --- |
| 1. Primary microcephaly; head circumference <3 S.D. below mean; sloping forehead, protruding ears | Autosomal recessive |
| 2. Primary hydrocephalus | Heterogenous |
| 3. Hydranencephaly and porencephaly | Sporadic |
| 4. Neural tube defects (includes anencephaly, spina bifida, encephalocele) | Heterogenous—majority are multifactorial |
| 5. Holoprosencephaly | Heterogenous; includes sporadic, AD, and AR forms |
| 6. Other malformation:<br><br>Dysgenesis-schizencephaly Agenesis, lissencephaly | Heterogenous; some sporadic, some AR, some X-linked. |

Table 3.6.  Multiple congenital anomaly/mental retardation syndromes—
selected examples

| Etiology | Disorder | Mode of inheritance |
|---|---|---|
| 1.  Known nonchromosomal syndromes: | Noonan syndrome | ?AD |
| | Rubinstein-Taybi syndrome | ?Sp |
| | Cornelia de Lange syndrome | ?Sp |
| | Smith-Lemli-Opita syndrome | AR |
| | Angelman syndrome | ?Sp |
| | Lowe syndrome | XR |
| 2.  Idiopathic, sporadic cases<br>Normal chromosomes<br>Unremarkable family history | | |
| 3.  Provisionally private syndromes<br>Do not fit a known recognizable syndrome<br>History of affected sibling<br>Normal chromosomes | | |

AD = autosomal dominant; Sp = sporadic; AR = autosomal recessive; XR = X-linked.

Dilantin syndrome and fetal alcohol syndrome. In regard to adults with mental retardation, particularly those on medication, for example, Dilantin for seizures, it would be helpful for genetic counseling to be provided. This enables optimal management during the pregnancy in terms of monitoring anticonvulsant medication. Also, certain teratogenic agents, such as alcohol, can be avoided. Reference has already been made to the teratogenic effects of phenylalanine in women with PKU.

## GENETIC EVALUATION

Genetic evaluation of a patient includes a detailed family history with pedigree analysis, past medical history, physical examination, and diagnostic workup. It is an essential prerequisite before any other genetic service can be provided. Accurate genetic counseling can only be provided after a thorough genetic evaluation has been attempted. Shown in Table 3.7 are the components of the evaluation of a patient in a genetics clinic (Berini & Kahn, 1987).

Table 3.7.  Components of genetic evaluation of a patient with mental retardation

History:
   Prenatal history
   Medical history
   Developmental history
   Family history and pedigree analysis

Physical Examination:
   Perusal of past medical records for confirmation of diagnosis and/or diagnostic procedures and tests on patient and other family members

Investigations (as necessary):
   Radiographic studies, including skull and skeletal films, CT scan, bone age
   Chromosome studies of peripheral blood or other tissue
   Fragile-X chromosomal preparation
   Blood and urine tests for amino acids; urine for organic acids and mucopolysaccharides; urine for reducing substances
   Serum electrolytes, ammonia, $CO_2$, blood glucose
   Serum uric acid
   Serum creatine phosphokinase
   Lysosomal enzyme analyses in blood, tears, platelets
   Muscle or tissue biopsy for histologic studies, including electron-microscopy and/or biochemical analysis
   Thyroid function tests
   Developmental and psychological testing
   Assessment of hearing and vision
   Electroencephalograms in awake and sleep states
   TORCH antibody titers (toxoplasmosis, rubella, cytomegalovirus, herpes)
   VDRL
   CSF (cerebrospinal fluid) analysis, including cultures

Referral to appropriate specialists

Genetic counseling

## GENETIC COUNSELING

The term genetic counseling is a misnomer in the sense that it is perceived by many to be a process in which the geneticist recommends or tells the patient and/or family what particular course of action to follow. As defined by the Ad Hoc Committee on Genetic Counseling of the American Society of Human Genetics:

> Genetic counseling is a communication process that deals with the human problems associated with the occurrence, or the risk of occurrence, of a genetic disorder in a family. This process involves an attempt by one or more appropriately trained persons to help the individual or family 1) comprehend the medical facts,

including the diagnosis, the probable course of the disorder, and the available management; 2) appreciate the way heredity contributes to the disorder and the risk of recurrence in specified relatives; 3) understand the options for dealing with the risk of recurrence; 4) choose the course of action that seems appropriate to them in view of their risk and the family goals, and act in accordance with that decision; and 5) make the best possible adjustment to the disorder in an affected family member and/or to the risk of recurrence of that disorder. (Epstein et al., 1975)

## RECURRENCE RISKS

Once a diagnosis has been established, the affected person and/or family can be counseled about the risk of recurrence according to the etiology and mode of inheritance for that particular disorder. When the etiology is not known, genetic counseling is done using empiric risks of recurrence, that is, figures obtained based only on observation of the recurrence of the defect in families once a proband has been identified. Present-

Table 3.8.  Empiric recurrence risk figures for mental retardation

| Type of union | Chance that the first child will have MR |
|---|---|
| 1. a  Person without MR (with MR sib) × person with MR | 23.8 |
| b  Person without MR (with MR sib) × person without MR | |
| i  First parent had only one MR sib | 1.8 ⎫ combined average = 2.5 |
| ii  First parent had two or more MR sibs | 3.6 ⎭ |
| 2.  Person without MR (all sibs without MR) × person without MR | 0.53 |

| Type of union | Number with MR after the first MR child (percent) |
|---|---|
| 1.  Person with MR × person with MR | 32 out of 76 (42.1%) |
| 2.  Person with MR × person without MR or unknown | 63 out of 317 (19.9%) |
| 3.  Person without MR × person without MR | |
| a  One parent without MR had one or more sibs with MR | 18 out of 139 (12.9%) |
| b  All sibs of one parent without MR known to be without MR | 6 out of 104 (5.7%) |

These risk figures are results of studies by Reed and Reed, 1965.

ed in Table 3.8 are empiric recurrence risk figures from studies by Reed and Reed (1965). Individuals with IQs less than 70 are included as having mental retardation. The risks are primarily those for milder mental retardation, although individuals with severe mental retardation are also included.

## SUMMARY

Mental retardation is of heterogenous etiology, including genetic as well as nongenetic causes. Genetic evaluation for etiology, management, and counseling is an integral component of modern medical care. An important factor is the recognition of different levels of mental retardation. The great majority of adults with mental retardation fall into the mild to moderate range of mental retardation and live in the community. Health care personnel need to realize that the offspring of these individuals do not necessarily have mental retardation and are more likely *not* to have mental disability. Genetic evaluation for etiology, management, and counseling is an integral component of modern medical care. It is important that all caregivers be aware of the need of adults with mental retardation and their family members for genetic evaluation and counseling. Mentally retarded adults in the community should be provided with comprehensive genetic services.

## REFERENCES

Baird, P., & Sadovnick, A. (1987). Life expectancy in down syndrome. *Journal of Pediatrics, 110*, 849–854.

Barker, D., Wright, E., & Nguyen, K. (1987). Gene for von Recklinghousen neurofibromatosis in the pericentromeric region of chromosome 17. *Science, 236*, 1100–1102.

Berini, R., & Kahn, E. (1987). *Clinical genetics handbook.* Oradell, New Jersey: Medical Economics Books.

DeGrouchy, J., & Turleau, C. (1984). *Clinical atlas of human chromosomes.* New York: John Wiley & Sons.

Elwood, J.L., & Darragh, P.M. (1981). Severe Mental Handicap in Northern Ireland. *Journal of Mental Deficiency Research, 25,* 147–155.

Emery, A.E.H., & Rimoin, D. (1983). *Principles and practice of medical genetics* (Vol. 1). Livingston, NY: Churchill.

Epstein, C., Childs, B., Fraser, F.C., McKusick, V., Miller, J., Motulsky, A., Rivas, M., Thompson, M., Shaw, M., & Sly, W. (1975). Genetic counseling. *American Journal of Human Genetics, 27,* 240–242.

Fryer, P., Conner, J., Povey, S., Yates, J., Chalmers, A., Fraser, I., Yates, A., & Osbourne, J. (1987). Evidence that the gene for tuberous sclerosis is on chromosome 9. *The Lancet, 1,* 659–660.

Fryers, T., & McKay, R. (1979). The epidemiology of severe mental handicap. *Early Human Development, 3,* 277–294.

Grossman, H.J. (Ed.). (1973). *Manual on terminology and classification in mental retardation.* Washington, DC: American Association on Mental Deficiency.

Grossman, H.J. (1977). *Manual on terminology and classification in mental retardation (American Association on Mental Deficiency Special Publication Series* No. 2). Baltimore: Garam and Pridemark Press.

Gustavson, K.H., Holmgren, G., Jonsell, R., & Son-Blomquist, H.K. (1977). Severe mental retardation in children in a northern Swedish county. *Journal of Mental Deficiency Research, 21,* 161–181.

Hagerman, R., Kemper, M., & Hudson, M. (1985). Learning disabilities and attentional problems in boys with the fragile X syndrome. *American Journal of Diseases of Children, 139,* 674–678.

Levy, H. (1985). *Maternal PKU. Medical genetics: Past, present, future.* New York: Alan R. Liss.

Lubs, H.A. (1969). A marker X chromosome. *American Journal of Human Genetics, 21,* 231.

McDonald, A.D. (1973). Severely retarded children in Quebec: Prevalence, causes and care. *American Journal of Mental Deficiency, 78,* 205–215.

McKusick, V.A. (1988). *Mendelian inheritance in man: Catalogs of autosomal dominant, autosomal recessive, and X-linked phenotypes* (8th ed.). Baltimore: Johns Hopkins University Press.

McLaren, J., & Bryson, S. (1987). Review of recent epidemiologic studies of mental retardation: Prevalence, associated disorders, and etiology. *American Journal of Mental Retardation, 92*(3), 243–254.

Niikawa, N., & Ishikiriyama, S. (1985). Clinical and cytogenetic studies of the Prader-Willi syndrome: Evidence of phenotype-karyotype correlation. *Human Genetics, 69,* 22–27.

Opitz, J. (1980). Mental retardation: Biological aspects of concern to pediatricians. *Pediatrics in Review, 2* (2), 41–43.

Opitz, J., Neri, G., Reynolds, J., & Spano, L. (1988). X-Linked mental retardation 3: Proceedings of the Third International Workshop on fragile X and X-linked Mental Retardation. *American Journal of Medical Genetics, 30.*

Reed, E., & Reed, S. (1965). *Mental retardation: A family study.* Philadelphia: W.B. Saunders.

Riccardi, V. (1981). Von Recklinghausen neurofibromatosis. *New England Journal of Medicine, 305,* 1617–1626.

Sherman, H., Morton, N., Jacobs, P., & Turner, G. (1984). The marker (X) syndrome: A cytogenetic and genetic analysis. *Annals of Human Genetics, 48,* 21–37.

Smith, D.W. (1988). *Recognizable patterns of human malformation.* Philadelphia: W.B. Saunders.

Thompson, J.S., & Thompson, M.W. (1986). *Genetics in Medicine* (4th ed.). New York: W.B. Saunders.

Turner, G., & Jacobs, P. (1983). Marker (X)-linked mental retardation. *Advances in Human Genetics, 13*, 83–112.

Turner, G., Robinson, H., Laing, S., & Purvis-Smith, S. (1986). Preventive screening for the fragile X syndrome. *New England Journal of Medicine, 315*, 607–609.

Watson, M.S., Leckman, J., Annex, B., Breg, W., & Boles, D. (1984). Fragile X in a survey of 75 autistic males. *New England Journal of Medicine, 310*, 1462.

Woo, S.L.C., Lidsky, A.S., & Guttler, F. (1984). Prenatal diagnosis of classical phenylketonuria by gene mapping. *Journal of the American Medical Association, 251*, 1989.

World Health Organization. (1980). *International classification of impairments, disabilities and handicaps.* Geneva: World Health Organization.

# III | Educational Interventions

# 4

# Parents Learning Together I

## Parenting skills training for adults with mental retardation

Barbara Y. Whitman
Betty Graves
Pasquale J. Accardo

**P**arental, especially maternal, mental retardation is a recognized risk factor for medical, emotional, and cognitive problems in children (Crain & Millor, 1978; Kaminer & Cohen, 1983; Sheridan, 1956). The principal contributing cause to the development of these problems does not appear to be either child abuse or a hereditary influence, but rather child neglect secondary to lack of parental education combined with the unavailability of supportive services (Schilling, Schinke, Blythe, & Barth, 1982; Seagull & Scheurer, 1986). A number of programs, including home and center based components, have been devised to address the educational issue (Gil & McKenna; Greenbaum & Noll, 1982; Parks, 1984). In an epidemiological survey, Whitman, Graves, and Accardo (1987) (a review of this study is included in Chapter 2) identified in the city of St. Louis 402 families headed by an adult with mental retardation and including from one to eight children. The impetus behind this study was a previous intensive clinical exposure to the multiple problems facing selected mentally retarded parents and their children. This experience uncovered a lack of both formal and informal community supports. The epidemiological study was therefore linked to a second pilot project to design a parent training program called Parents Learning Together (PLT) for adults who have mental retardation and to attempt to assess its impact (Graves, Graves, Haynes, Rice, & Whitman, 1986; Whitman, Graves, & Accordo, in press). Chapter 4 provides an overview of the program's design, a description of the families served, selected outcome data, and some of the problems encountered.

## PARTICIPANTS

The program was advertised directly to the agencies participating in the concurrent case finding study and through the local media. Client referrals came mainly from Regional Center caseworkers, the Division of Family Services (DFS), social workers at Cardinal Glennon Children's Hospital, and other pediatric services in the city of St. Louis. The program was free to participants. Family criteria for entry into PLT included: 1) a parental intelligence quotient (IQ) of 69 or less, 2) residence in the city of St. Louis, and 3a) at least one preschool child in the home, or 3b) a mother with mental retardation who was pregnant. Parental IQ screening with the Slosson Intelligence Test—Revised (SIT-R) (Slosson, 1985) was completed prior to acceptance into the program. However, in most cases, previous IQ scores were available and served as the basis for identification and referral. Selected characteristics of the 23 families served during the first year of the program are presented in Table 4.1. While the adults with mental retardation were the targeted focus of the

Table 4.1.   Family size and parent descriptors

| Number of children | 1 | 2 | 3 | 4 | | 5 | | 6 | |
|---|---|---|---|---|---|---|---|---|---|
| Families | 5 | 5 | 8 | 2 | | 0 | | 3 | |

| | | Age | | IQ | | Distribution | | |
|---|---|---|---|---|---|---|---|---|
| | N | Mean | Range | Mean | Range | 50 | 50–60 | 60 |
| Female | 23 | 27.7 | 17–41 | 50.6 | 35–69 | 6 | 14 | 3 |
| Male | 3 | 24.0 | 22–28 | 55.0 | 50–65 | 0 | 2 | 1 |

The average number of children per family was 2.57 with a range of 1–6. In addition to these 65 children, two of the mothers were pregnant. No age ranges are given for the children because parents were not always certain of their ages or the number of older children who had previously been removed from the home.

intervention, the hands-on teaching strategy required them to bring to the program at least one of their preschool children. At some time during the year, each of these 28 children was administered either an SIT-R or the Griffiths Mental Development Scales (Griffiths, 1970, 1976). Two thirds of the children tested in the broad normal range of intelligence, and all scores were clinically considered underestimates of true ability. There was no meaningful correlation between adult IQ, child IQ, or adult PLT performance.

## PROGRAM DEVELOPMENT

As we began to plan for our parenting program we spent many brainstorming sessions and gave much thought to the form that the delivery system should take. Ultimately, we decided on a center-based program with a home component that included one or two home visits weekly. The basic teaching would take place at the center, while home visits would allow staff to assess how well learning was being generalized to the home situation.

Our rationale for selecting this model was based on seven points:

1.  Several parents with mental retardation who had children already being served at the parent Early Childhood Speech Education program had occasionally attended same parent meetings. We were aware of and touched by their obvious hunger for social contact.
2.  Peer pressure can often contribute to learning. We knew at least two parents with mental retardation who would be participating in the pilot project and who would be positive influences.
3.  Some of the basic areas to be taught could be better supervised in a group setting.
4.  Some of the PLT children could be integrated into existing preschool classes since they were housed in the same building and close enough to be pulled out for parent-child interactions.
5.  PLT families could be added to United States Department of Agriculture contract and could thus receive a balanced, nutritious breakfast and lunch.
6.  Our center was located within a half block of Cardinal Glennon Children's Hospital, a tertiary level university teaching facility, where PLT children could receive any needed care.

7. That home visits could begin after 2 or 3 weeks of center programming would make it easier for clients to accept staff visits in their homes.

With the basic service delivery system decided upon, we began to plan how to program for key problem areas.

As professionals with backgrounds in early childhood, special education, social work, and health care, we did not begin this program with our eyes closed. All of us had worked with poverty level, inner city families. We knew the existing service delivery system did not work well for most such families. We knew that the health care delivery system was far from infallible. Many working persons with incomes at the poverty level had no medical insurance and no other resources to pay for health care. We were well acquainted with the substandard housing available to poor persons. We knew that, while food stamps helped, they often left "hungry days" at the month's end. We had all had varying degrees of professional involvement with parents who had mental retardation, so we were aware of the extra coping problems that came with mental disabilities.

Even so, we discovered quickly that our ideas about an appropriate curriculum for parents with mental retardation would need to change drastically. We had read several parenting curricula for persons identified as having mental retardation and discovered that, in those curricula, the mentally retarded parents were much closer to the borderline range than our clients. Clients in the other programs ranged in IQ from the 70s to the 80s. In contrast, we were dealing with clients whose intellectual functioning ranged from the high 60s downward. Most were in the low to mid-50s, with some in the 40s. Our curriculum and expectations could not be the same as for the clients in the other programs. In our planning and thinking we saw child care (both personal and medical) and parent-child relationships as the major areas to be covered. We knew, too, that we would need to give elementary level guidance on the basics of home management and food preparation. What we did not envision was that we would be dealing with persons with mental retardation who never had received any or had received none or very few services while growing up. They had little skill in caring for themselves, much less in caring for children. We found that we had to go back to the drawing board again and again. Hygiene care of the child involved hygiene habits for both parents and children. Home management and food preparation assumed greater importance. Still more time needed to be spent on helping parents learn to interact with their infants and young children. We had seen child management as a necessary ingredient of the curriculum, but again the reality far overshadowed our expectations.

As we began to program and came to know our clients, many of the theoretical characteristics of adults with mental retardation were seen in real life. The following vignette illustrates how some of these characteristics came alive for us as we worked with the mentally retarded parents in our program.

> Frequently parents with mental retardation see infants as "dolls" to be played with—or not—as dictated by the parents', and not the infant's, needs. Many have little or no understanding that they are relating to another human being. They may handle their infant as they would an inanimate object. Nellie was 21 and had a 2-year-old girl and 8-month-old Jerry. Jerry was a placid, almost withdrawn, baby. He made sounds only occasionally and played with toys in an indifferent manner. His mother met his physical needs in an equally indifferent fashion. He was given food at appropriate intervals; his diapers were changed less frequently than desirable, but often enough to keep diaper rash at bay— most of the time. Watching Nellie change his diaper was like watching a clerk wrap a lumpy package. There were no words or comforting sounds, no eye contact; it was just a matter of getting the job done. When Janet, the parent aide assigned to Nellie, began modeling more appropriate diapering behavior, Nellie said to Janet, "Why you talk him? He don't understand and he don't say nuthin." The aide responded briefly that babies need attention and that hearing people talk to him would encourage him to make sounds and eventually talk. Nellie was unconvinced. Gradually, though, we began to see some slight differences as Nellie changed Jerry. Then one day, with a smiling Jerry in her arms, a jubilant Nellie announced to all that Jerry *did* understand. "I talk to him; he make noises back! He love me!"

Seeing babies as human beings who thrive on interaction is, at first, hard for many adults with mental retardation to grasp. Changing the pattern is difficult, but patience and repetition *can* make a difference. The best teacher is the baby himself or herself. When the baby begins to respond by smiling and cooing, the parent feels good and gives the baby more attention, and the interaction and stimulation go on, creating a bond between parent and child.

## RESULTS

All adults with mental retardation who participated in the PLT program were given a battery of tests for the purpose of providing a baseline instructional level and also to determine the need for further referrals to medical and allied health services in the community. Components of the test battery included the Communicative Abilities in Daily Living (Holland, 1980); a speech and language assessment; a hearing screening (pure tone audiometry and middle ear functioning); a dental examination (through the Elk's Dental Clinic at Washington University, St. Louis, MO); a parent-child interaction analysis (turn-taking: type, number, and appropriateness of responses over a 5-minute observation period); and an informal assessment of the emotional functioning of the parent. A physical evaluation screened height, weight, blood pressure, and resting pulse rate, and a physical therapy assessment looked at posture, muscle strength, and joint range of motion. The HOME (Home Observation for the Measurement of the Environment) scale (Caldwell & Bradley) was administered during the initial home visit in the first year of the program, but its use was discontinued after that because the high rate of socially desirable responses (the clients tended to tell us what they thought we wanted to hear) rendered the resulting profile inaccurate. With this information collected, the PLT staff met with representatives of participating agencies and other involved professionals to formulate an individualized education program (IEP) for each participant. The curriculum did not utilize strict behavior modification or task analysis but was derived mainly from a cognitively oriented approach (Weikert, Hohmann, & Banet, 1979). With each successive repetition following a Plan-Do-Recall model, the mentally retarded parent assumed responsibility for a progressively larger part of the sequence. This tactic actually seemed to improve performance even when the parent was unable to completely verbalize the sequence. Results for selected IEP areas are presented in Table 4.2. (The IEP format was utilized throughout the first year of the PLT program. In the second year it was replaced with a contract format in order to give the clients a greater sense of control over setting learning objectives.)

All families made progress in selected parenting skills. Because the families would continue to receive varying degrees of agency and community support services, no attempt was made to arrive at a global parenting adequacy score. No specific intake variable correlated with degree of improvement in parenting skills, with one possible exception. The two families that both made the greatest progress and exhibited the best reten-

Table 4.2.  Achievement of selected IEP goals

| IEP Area | Number of goals | Number of parents (average) | Percent completed |
|---|---|---|---|
| Parent-child interaction | 4 | 8 | 75 |
| Medical care | 9 | 5 | 53 |
| Personal hygiene | 4 | 8 | 50 |
| Money management | 3 | 4 | 55 |

The varying number of parents for each goal reflects the individualization of goal setting to the baseline functional level of each adult with mental retardation.

tion of that progress were the ones who started with and seemed best able to utilize the existing network of support services, including their own extended families. A long-term follow-up on the continued placement and progress of the children in these 23 families will need to be performed.

Most of the mentally retarded parents entered the program with poor self esteem. They did not see themselves as important to the program or to others. With these twin facts in mind we worked hard to establish a group for these parents to obtain a sense of belonging, as well as a sense of responsibility to the group. One of our first pieces of evidence that this was beginning to work came from a client named Margo:

> We had talked about planning a Halloween party for the PLT children. With the excitement of a little girl, Margo said she would bake a cake! We accepted her offer and said we would remind her a few days before the event. Two days later (a full 3 weeks before the party) Margo presented the cake for our approval. It was flat and very sad looking. The sickly green icing only made it worse. It resembled nothing so much as a green brick. Margo's dancing eyes helped us hold at bay our appalled feelings. We thanked her profusely and admired the culinary masterpiece held out for our inspection. Reminding Margo that the event was 3 weeks in the future, we offered to freeze the cake. Unfortunately Margo could not be separated from her prize and said she would bring it back at the appointed time. Bring it back she did, flatter and sicklier looking than before. Margo's self esteem hung in the balance. It took some fancy choreography to see that Margo's cake was admired by all and devoured by none! We added cake baking to our list of future lesson plans.

Successfully working with mothers who have mental retardation meant that we had to be sure never to underestimate the power and influence wielded by the man in their lives. For women who had had little love and nurturance, the man was extremely important. They needed his love and attention, however spasmodic and unreliable it was. In some cases, the man drifted in and out of their lives. The man's interest and involvement with the children varied from open resentment and no interaction (if not overt abuse) to obvious love and participation in their care. In our case load, most of the men functioned between a level of mental retardation and a borderline normal level. For example, consider Brent, whose IQ was in the mid-50s.

> Brent ruled his family absolutely. Two of the three children were his biological children. He insisted that the eldest was also his, but the family history strongly indicated otherwise. Brent was the original male chauvinist. His wife Ellie was totally subservient to him. There was a strict sexist delineation of responsibilities in the family. He made the decisions—she carried out his orders. The youngest child was 3 months old when Brent and his family entered PLT. They came because their attendance was a condition of getting physical custody of the 3-month-old who had been placed in foster care at birth. The Division of Family Services (DFS) had been involved on behalf of the older children, and conditions in the home were such that the newborn was placed in foster care. The 3-month-old was returned to their care, and their attendance and cooperation in PLT was monitored for 6 months before DFS closed the case. Brent functioned at a higher cognitive level than did Ellie. He saw his duty as keeping track of household and child tasks and seeing that Ellie carried out the work. As the work and activities at PLT went on, Brent would announce imperiously: "One O'clock—Ellie go feed Jimmy." Or, "11:00 O'clock— Ellie change diapers," and quickly Ellie complied. The staff felt that a real success had been achieved the day Brent bathed his baby at the center and actually showed some tenderness as he cared for the little boy. Brent never came even close to accepting equal parenting chores with Ellie, but he did begin to take on more direct responsibility than before.

The overinvolvement or underinvolvement of extended family made a strong impact in the lives of our clients and on their participation in the program. For some parents with mental retardation who had little or no contact with their own parents and siblings, there was a sense of isolation and abandonment. In some cases our clients had literally been set adrift as young teens by rejecting families. They felt the rejection keenly and drew the conclusion that they were not worth the love and care of a family. Some of these parents came to PLT reluctantly, with no expectation of warmth or acceptance. They maintained their isolation in the midst of people and rejected overtures from others. Some latched on to individual staff members in an effort to find the love, nurturance, and attention they had been denied.

Difficult as it was to meet the needs of these clients, even more roadblocks stood in the way when the staff worked with clients with overinvolved families. In a few cases, the adult parents of our clients were a positive influence, serving as good role models and willing to give needed support to both their adult children and to the grandchildren. Unfortunately, this was not the usual situation. In most cases with involved extended families, the influence was negative.

Some of our clients were viewed exclusively as "paychecks" by their relatives. Others were treated as unpaid servants. Following is an example of such a situation.

> Jane, who was mentally retarded, had three children and was pregnant. She was expected to do the washing and cleaning for herself, her husband, her children, her mother-in-law, her mother-in-law's live-in boyfriend and often one or two of her husband's friends who moved in for weeks at a time. This household lived on Jane's Supplemental Social Security Income check, which went to the mother-in-law, and a few dollars from her husband's Social Security check. James, Jane's husband, who also had mental retardation, regarded Jane's check as "live-on money." His check was designated for more important things such as pop-rock sweat shirts, additions to his pipe collection, and $100 boots. Jane loved coming to the program and picked up on the parenting lectures quickly. Unfortunately, her mother-in-law disparaged "the silly junk" she was learning, and, of course, James agreed with his mother, who had raised six children.

One of the more difficult aspects of working with parents who have mental retardation is their strong tendency to become very dependent on the help of one or more of their professional workers. They seem to need to assure themselves that the professional *cares* and *will respond.* The usual ways of avoiding unhealthy dependency never seem to work as well with clients who have mental retardation. Part of the problem lies in their constant crisis orientation. From food stamps running out to needed plumbing repairs, from "dangerously" ill children to Division of Family Services warnings that they must move from apartments with high lead levels, nothing has any lead-in time. The problem for the helping professional is to know when the crisis is immediate and when a delay of a day or two will make little significant difference.

> One of our most crisis-oriented and dependent clients was Patrice. It was a rare day when no crisis loomed on her horizon. Knowing that she lived with her brother and his domineering girlfriend, the staff were inclined to respond quickly when Patrice sounded any alarm. Late night calls were not uncommon. Often

the crisis could be resolved over the telephone. On responding to one 10:00 p.m. call made from a street telephone booth, the worker found Patrice and her two small children standing shivering near the telephone booth. This was no false alarm. While her brother was at work, Patrice had been locked out of the house by his girlfriend for a reason neither she nor staff were ever able to discover. Telephone calls to her brother at work and a conversation through the door with the girlfriend finally ended the locked door policy, and quiet returned for a time. Other alarms were more annoying and less important. Once when a tired PLT staff member attempted to go to her rescue at 1:00 a.m., she was not where she said she would be. Alarmed, the staff member went to her apartment to see if her brother knew anything. The door was opened by a nightgown-clad Patrice who calmly stated, "Everything's OK now." False alarms or real crisis alarms, with Patrice one never knew.

Janet, who had an IQ in the mid-60s, kept her children reasonably clean and neat, but medical appointments and having herself and her children ready for PLT when the bus came in the morning were entirely different matters. Her excuses ranged far and wide, but as staff worked with her, the real problem soon became apparent. She had no alarm clock to wake her, and, once awake, she had no idea when the bus would come. A large calendar with medical appointment days circled and daily crossing off of days helped. An alarm clock set so she woke up and had time to get downstairs for the bus helped too. She understood that the exact time for going downstairs was "when the big hand is on 5 and the little hand, on 7." A PLT worker made reminder calls for medical appointments and gave her "big hand-little hand" instructions for leaving home. Janet's dependability in keeping medical appointments and getting to PLT became routine.

## DISCUSSION

Parents with mental retardation are first and foremost adults with mental retardation. The specific problems encountered in attempting to teach parenting skills were direct reflections of the limitations in adaptive behavior and social skills observed in adults who have mental retardation. Typical problems included speech and language disorders; difficulties with organizing, sequencing, and adhering to time schedules; overgeneralization and undergeneralization; low self-esteem; previously undiagnosed hearing loss; dental emergency (80%); homelessness (46% in one year); previous and current history of abuse; inability to read social and nonverbal cues; a tendency for recurrent crises to overtax and ultimately burn out existing social supports; and themselves becoming a focus of contention among multiple agencies.

Despite the provision of transportation, attendance was sporadic and fluctuated around 50% of enrolled clients on any one day. (The switch to a token economy later improved the absenteeism rate.) With approximately half the families, compliance was taken into account in decisions by the Division of Protective Services on disposition of children, and this improved attendance. In only one case were the PLT staff compelled to support removal of three children from an abusive family with two higher functioning parents who had mental retardation.

Success and failure occurred in varying amounts. Along with appreciating the successes, we certainly learned from the failures. As we look back on our experience, we can put the successes and failures in better perspective. To say that the deck is stacked against parents with mental retardation is an understatement.

These parents are faced with a set of circumstances that make daily living extremely difficult. Many are single parents. Most live in substandard housing with poor to nonexistent plumbing arrangements. The family income is usually some combination of Supplemental Social Security Income, Aid to Dependent Children, and food stamps. In most cases this translates into a total amount that places them below the poverty level. In addition to being head-of-household for one to eight children, many also have one or more parents, grandparents, or friends who have moved in and who rarely have any income of their own. Often they do not even contribute any work to the household. Given this set of circumstances, it is hard to imagine even parents who do not have mental disabilities mustering the day-to-day stamina needed.

Working with parents who have mental retardation is difficult in the extreme. The disorganization of every facet of their lives, as well as their inability to understand many everyday givens, can be frustrating beyond belief. Their unrelenting 24-hours-a-day needs, wants, and demands make professional burnout an ever-present specter.

Not every client was willing or capable of learning to use acceptable parenting techniques. When we stood by as children were placed in foster care, we felt like failures even though we agreed such placement was necessary for the safety and emotional well-being of the child. After a time we came to accept that intervention with mentally retarded parents and their children could have more than one successful outcome. For the parents who were motivated and intellectually capable of learning to be good parents, improved parent-child relationship and better child care would be the happy result. For parents who were unmotivated or intellectually incapable of carrying out necessary routines, the removal and appropriate placement of the child would be the necessary outcome and could also be seen as success. We, as professionals, failed only when we did not accept the obvious and advocate for the needed interventions and outcomes.

With all the problems and difficulties, there remain some outstanding successes. One of our most frustrating clients was a mother whose motivation waxed and waned, but she is now completing her GED at the age of 36. Some of our clients who had been isolated and friendless found friends among their peers in the program. Some developed solid friendships, visiting back and forth and baby-sitting for one another. They reinforced each other in the skills they had learned, and they continue to improve the quality-of-life for each other.

Another mother, who had spent 20 years in an abusive marriage and lost six children to Division of Family Services because of the paternal child abuse, found the courage to leave that situation and begin again. Another couple, Bertha and Jason, worked hard at changing their parenting practices. To escape negative extended family intervention, they moved to a rural community and continue to do well with no public support.

A given cognitive level of functioning is neither required nor sufficient for adequate parenting. Leo Kanner (1949, pp. 4–5) wrote, "In my 20 years of psychiatric work with thousands of children and their parents, I have seen percentally at least as many 'intelligent' adults unfit to rear their offspring as I have seen such 'feebleminded' adults. I have . . . come to the conclusion that to a large extent independent of the I.Q., fitness for parenthood is determined by emotional involvements and relationships." Our experience with PLT supports this observation that the capacity to give appropriate love, care, nurturance, and emotional involvement is not predictable on the basis of IQ alone. Otherwise, there would be no parents who do not have mental disabilities who are guilty of child abuse and neglect.

However, for adults with mental retardation to be effective parents, additional educational support and other long-term support for those aspects of parenting that have cognitive prerequisites may be necessary. There may also exist a point at which the degree of mental retardation demands such a high level of support as to threaten the practicality, in a given case (and not on the basis of IQ), of parenting. But the existence and location of that cutoff point needs to be proven and not presumed. A doctrine of fairness does not allow mentally retarded parents to be treated differently from parents who do not have mental retardation and who neglect, abuse, and otherwise mistreat their children (Friedman, 1976, p. 182). It is not that any parent, with mental retardation or not, has any right to mistreat children, rather that parents who are having difficulties with childrearing should be able to expect from the community a certain amount of support services to help compensate for their deficiencies. Such support services must target the needs of specific populations. Current Division of Family Services-sponsored parenting classes typically are not geared toward parents who have mental retardation. Although more than two thirds of parents with mental retardation perceive learning, behavior, and medical problems in their children, fewer than 15% are able to locate any sort of usable support. Principal societal intervention is for half to be reported for abuse and neglect and a quarter to have a child removed from the home (Whitman et al., 1987).

PLT and similar programs can improve the parenting skills of mentally retarded adults with their preschool children. The teaching of such skills is not a routine component of current special education curricula. There are no studies of the long-term impact on the child or the mentally retarded parent of fostering such improved skills. The question of whether the parenting skills of adults with significant mental retardation can be sufficiently developed to respond to the emotional needs and other psychosocial developmental requirements of school-age children and adolescents is exceedingly problematic. The feasibility or desirability of adopting both the child and the mentally retarded parent into another family or a group home setting, as an alternative to termination of parental rights, also remains unexplored.

When a female minor becomes a parent, she is considered legally emancipated. When an adult female with mental retardation has a child, she is often de facto emancipated from the existing support service network for adults with mental retardation for the simple reason that parenting is not a recognized potential outcome for such a person. Although there are no reliable statistics as to whether the numbers of persons with mental retardation who are having children are increasing or decreasing, this unrecognized population and its untreated problems will not go away. Society must somehow come to accept the reality that their situation will not go away. Children are being born to parents with mental retardation every day. These parents must be given support and guidance from day one if both the parents and children are to lead productive lives.

## REFERENCES

Caldwell, B., & Bradley, R. *Home observation for measurement of the environment: HOME manual.* Little Rock: Center for Child Development University of Arkansas at Little Rock, Arkansas.

Crain, L.S., & Millor, G.K. (1978). Forgotten children: Maltreated children of mentally retarded parents. *Pediatrics, 61,* 130–132.

Friedman, P.R. (Ed.) (1976). *The rights of mentally retarded persons.* New York: Avon Books.

Gil, L., & McKenna, D. *Parenting skills curriculum: A curriculum for mentally handicapped parents of young children.* Seattle, Washington: Northwest Center Infant Development Program.

Graves, B., Graves, D., Haynes, Y., Rice, G.B., & Whitman, B.Y. (1986). *Parents Learning Together: A curriculum for use with MR/DD parents.* St. Louis: St. Louis Office for MR/DD Resources.

Greenbaum, M., & Noll, S.J. (1982). *Education for adulthood: A curriculum for the mentally retarded who need a better understanding of life's processes and a training guide for those who will teach the curriculum.* Staten Island, New York: Staten Island Mental Health Society/Center for Developmental Disabilities.

Griffiths, R. (1970). The abilities of young children: *A comprehensive system of mental measurement for the first eight years of life.* London: Child Development Research Center.

Griffiths, R. (1976). *The abilities of babies: A study in mental measurement.* London: Association for Research in Infant and Child Development.

Holland, A.L. (1980). *Communicative abilities in daily living: A test of functional communication for aphasic adults.* Austin, Texas: PRO-ED.

Kaminer, R.K., & Cohen, H.J. (1983). Intellectually limited mothers. In *Developmental handicaps: Prevention and treatment.* (pp. 24–44). Washington, D.C.: AAUAP (American Association of University Affiliated Programs for Persons with Developmental Disabilities).

Kanner, L. (1949). *A miniature textbook of feeblemindedness.* New York: Child Care Publications.

Parks, S. (Ed.). (1984). *Help: When the parent is handicapped.* Palo Alto, California: VORT Corporation.

Schilling, R.F., Schinke, S.P., Blythe, B.J., & Barth, R.P. (1982). Child maltreatment and mentally retarded parents: Is there a relationship? *Mental Retardation, 20,* 201–209.

Seagull, E.A.W., & Scheurer, S.L. (1986). Neglected and abused children of mentally retarded parents. *Child Abuse & Neglect, 10,* 493–500.

Sheridan, M.D. (1956). The intelligence of 100 neglectful mothers. *British Journal of Medicine, 1,* 91–92.

Slosson, R. (1985). *The Slosson Intelligence Test for Children and Adults.* East Aurora, New York: Slosson Educational Publications.

Weikert, D.P., Hohmann, M., & Banet, B. (1979). *The cognitively oriented curriculum.* Ypsilanti, MI: HIgh Scope Educational Foundation.

Whitman, B.Y., Graves, B., & Accardo, P.J. (1987). The mentally retarded parent in the community: Identification method and needs assessment survey. *American Journal of Mental Deficiency, 91,* 636–638.

Whitman, B.Y., Graves, B., & Accardo, P.J. (in press). Parenting skills training for adults with mental retardation. *Social Work.*

# 5 Parents Learning Together II

## Selected modules from the curriculum

Betty Graves
David Graves
Yvonne Haynes
Gale Rice
Barbara Y. Whitman

## MODULE 1: CHILD DEVELOPMENT

### BACKGROUND

Young children are egocentric. Too often this is misinterpreted as selfishness. The reality is that a young child is incapable of seeing from any point of view other than his or her own. The child experiences himself or herself as the center of the world. Persons and situations are important only as they have an impact on him or her. Something akin to this egocentricity of early childhood continues to be operant in the lives of many adults with mental retardation. This perspective adds difficulty to the task of helping parents with mental retardation learn and understand the needs and capabilities of their young children. Egocentricity may be one of the reasons for which parents with mental retardation interpret many normal child be-

This chapter is adapted from Graves, B., Graves, D., Haynes, Y., Rice, G.B., and Whitman, B. (1986). *Parents learning together: A curriculum for use with MR/DD parents.* St. Louis: St. Louis Office for MR/DD Resources.

haviors (e.g., crying, needing diaper change) as directed *against* them. Another stumbling block is that parents with mental retardation have less knowledge and information about child development than do parents who do not have mental retardation. Without this basic understanding, parents who have mental retardation tend to have unrealistic expectations for their children, so they often interpret normal behaviors with the attitude, "She's just bad," or "He's doing that just to make me mad."

One mother with mental retardation who thought her 3-month-old should be ready for three meals a day became angry at the hungry, crying, screaming infant who "was yelling for no reason." One mentally retarded father thought his baby should sleep whenever he was put in his crib. When this did not happen, the father became angry and yelled at the baby. Predictably, the frightened infant cried louder. Another couple with mental retardation allowed their 15-month-old to stay in wet or soiled diapers for long periods of time because he had not cooperated with their goal of toilet training by 12 months of age. "He needs learn!" they would say.

It could be argued that all of these examples indicate emotional and physical abuse or at least neglect. Undeniably, without professional intervention, severe abuse or removal of the children would have been the likely outcome. New information and professional support allowed parents the understanding and courage to make changes. Intervention made a difference.

Module 1 not only includes information about the developmental changes that occur as children grow, but also addresses the need for change in child management techniques from stage to stage. This module requires a variety of lesson plans throughout the year to address these changes. Intensive teaching/learning will be based both at the center and at home. Some of the lessons will be taught within small groups; many will be on a one-to-one basis.

As important as specific targeted sessions with the clients will be, day-to-day modeling by the professional staff may provide the best teaching. As parents with mental retardation observe staff members setting limits and maintaining them as the need arises, the parents' skills will grow.

## GOALS AND OBJECTIVES

Goal:   Parents develop an understanding of normal child developmental sequences as they relate to discipline. Figure 5.1

| | | | | |
|---|---|---|---|---|
| 1. | Babies should be toilet trained by 12 months. | True | False | Don't Know |
| 2. | Up until 12 months, the only care a baby needs is to be fed, diapered, and bathed. | True | False | Don't Know |
| 3. | Babies cry to exercise their lungs. | True | False | Don't Know |
| 4. | Baby can be kept in the crib except when being fed or bathed. | True | False | Don't Know |
| 5. | It's not important to talk to baby until he or she begins to use words. | True | False | Don't Know |
| 6. | Young children do not need snacks between meals. | True | False | Don't Know |
| 7. | Picture books are good for children 9 months to 2 years old. | True | False | Don't Know |
| 8. | Two-year-olds should not be allowed to use crayons. | True | False | Don't Know |
| 9. | By age 2½, children should never have toilet accidents. | True | False | Don't Know |
| 10. | Two-year-olds should be punished if they do not share. | True | False | Don't Know |
| 11. | Watching TV is good for young children. | True | False | Don't Know |
| 12. | Children need a special time with Mother and/or Father before bed. | True | False | Don't Know |
| 13. | Young children should not be allowed to ask questions when parents are working around the house. | True | False | Don't Know |

Figure 5.1.    Pretest/Posttest for Module 1: Child Development.

shows a test to be administered to parents before and, again, after Module 1.

Objective 1.   To demonstrate appropriate disciplinary measures for a given child in a given role-playing situation, with 90% accuracy

Objective 2.   To demonstrate appropriate disciplinary measures for a given child during free play during 3 out of 4 data collection days

Objective 3.   To demonstrate appropriate parent responses requiring judgment of age-appropriate versus age-inappropriate behaviors during role-playing, with 90% accuracy

## SAMPLE SESSION

This session will be presented only after time is spent going over the developmental characteristics of children at ages 1–2 months, 2–4 months, 4–6 months, 6–9 months, 9–12 months, 1 year, 2 years, 3 years, and 4 years (Figure 5.2).

### Large Group Discussion

Group Leader: "We've been talking about what our pre-schoolers are like. For example, look at our picture chart about

---

**Birth to Two Months**

Pauses when hears a new sound
Stares at close objects
Likes to be moved place to place as parent goes about household tasks
Sleeps many hours a day

---

**2–4 Months**

When lying on stomach, baby lifts head and chest
If held standing up, lifts one foot
Learns to balance head
Rolls over
Watches own hands
Puts objects in mouth
Reaches for objects
Makes simple sounds "ah-eh-uh"
Coos
Looks directly at you
Chuckles
Turns head to voice or other sounds
Recognizes familiar face
Recognizes bottle
Smiles

---

*(continued)*

Figure 5.2.   How children grow. (Adapted from e.g., Accardo & Capute, 1979; Illingworth, 1967; Sheridan, 1968.)

Figure 5.2   (*continued*)

## 4–6 Months

Stands holding on
Picks up cube
Has a better hold on rattle
Lifts cup with handle
"Locates" sound
"Talks" to self in mirror
Reacts to seeing a toy
Realizes someone is a stranger and is unsure about strangers
Turns head to see dropped object
Plays peek-a-boo
Picks up spoon
Responds to attention with smiles and laughs
Feeds self a cracker
Sits up alone

## 6–9 Months

Shows interest in people
Cries when parent leaves room
Responds to others:
   Laughs when others laugh
   Cries at threatening gestures or angry voices
Holds toys—plays actively with rattle
Smiles at self in mirror—pats mirror
Watches everything, especially movement
Can amuse self 15 minutes at a time
Listens to own voice
Says "Dada," "Mama," with no particular meaning
Stops when hears "No, no"

(*continued*)

2s and 3s. Remember, we decided they were active, curious, talkative, need time with mom and dad, and like messy play (Playdoh, sand, water). Now we are ready to think about what rules or limits need to be set at home for playtimes. We'll talk

Figure 5.2    (*continued*)

---

**9–12 Months**

Plays pat-a-cake; waves bye-bye
More shy with "outsiders"
Repeats action that gets a laugh
Bangs toys together
Splashes in tub, crumples paper
Shakes rattle
Likes to put objects into and pull objects out of containers
Holds, bites, and chews cookie
Finger feeds part of meal
May extend arm or leg to be dressed
Rubs spoon across plate and licks spoon
Responds to "No, no"
Makes noises to get attention
Uses a few words (Mama and Dada) meaningfully
Claps hands on request
Jabbers with expression
Responds to own name
Indicates wants
Imitates some familiar words

---

(*continued*)

about other parts of the daily routine and limits on an-other day."

The group is divided into smaller groups of no more than three family units, and one staff member.

### Small Group Activity

Each small group will describe existing play arrangements in the home for their preschool children. They will discuss where toys are kept, how accessible they are to the children, where and when the children may play and what limits need to be maintained. Families with more than one preschool-age child will need help in working out plans that take each child's indi-vidual needs into account. Much time will be spent helping the parent find specific ways of meeting needs. For example, one

Figure 5.2  (*continued*)

---

**1–2 Years**

Walks
Holds two small objects in one hand
Walks up and down stairs with one hand held
Jumps in place
Recognizes people
Scribbles on paper
Recognizes family member names
Enjoys music, rocks whole body rhythmically
Jabbers, sounds like talking
Names pictures in a book
May use 20 or more words
Uses words and gestures to get what wants
Uses two words together
Points to three body parts, names body parts on demand
Demands to feed self
Pulls off socks, mittens
Eats with a spoon
Drinks from a cup
Tries to wash self
Offers toy but snatches it back
Helps with simple jobs
Plays alone happily if near adults

---

(*continued*)

parent could be very nurturing with her two children during some daily routines but during playtime she expected them to keep busy and permitted no breaks for hugs or comfort. Within the small group, the staff member will help each family unit identify appropriate limits for each of their children. Role-playing will be done for possible play situations.

## Large Group Sharing

When the total group reconvenes, the leader will provide opportunity for the parents to discuss what just happened. Acceptance and positive reinforcement will need to be given liberally.

Figure 5.2    (*continued*)

**Two Years Old**

Walking, *not* toddling

Vocabulary: The number of words understood and used is growing rapidly

Favorite words are "No" and "Mine" and represent attempt to control own world

Plays solitarily but also enjoys being around other children

Does not understand sharing and should not be punished for not sharing; parent should simply provide enough toys for all

**Three Years Old**

Anxious to please; loves to do what "Mommy says"

Can play with another child and can share some of the time

Likes parents to share play; likes to help with dishes, vacuuming, and so forth

Runs

Play becomes more imaginative

Enjoys story times

Increasing self-control

Verbal aggression and threats

**Four Years Old**

Developing control and coordination

"Runs away"

Kicks, spits, out-of-bounds behavior in every direction

Counts three or four objects

Less anxious to please or conform

Brags, shows off possessions

Tells tall tales with little distinction between true and false

Parents will need to be reassured that more help will follow. They should be reminded that parenting staff members will help with the task of knowing each child's needs and setting appropriate limits during home visits.

## Information Parents Need

Parents who have mental retardation need to know that the abilities of infants and young children are always changing. They must learn that their own expectations of their child's behavior also need to change in order to fit the child's developing capabilities. Parents of every intellectual level are concerned about discipline.

Limits are essential to ensure the safety and security of the child, as well as to help meet the needs of mentally retarded parents. For a young child, *security* is based on having things happen in the same way every day and in having today's "No's" be tomorrow's "No's." If the child jumps on Mother's bed, that's a "No" yesterday, today, and tomorrow. Rules need to be consistent. The limit, then, is: jump on the floor. No jumping on Mother's bed.

Limits on the child's behavior must also be based on what parents can reasonably live with. Having the child use a quiet, indoor voice may be important to one parent but not to another. Though some of the limits set for the child may seem to be only for the parents' benefit, this may not necessarily be the only benefit. Anything that helps the parents cope ultimately benefits the child.

Discipline and punishment are two separate things. Discipline is setting reasonable limits and providing the control the child does not yet have. A situation involving safety provides an example: A child is throwing toys and the parent steps in (perhaps physically holding child) and says, "Toys are to play with. Let's see how high you can build a block tower." This is discipline: setting a reasonable limit.

Punishment might be a spanking or removal of the toy without helping the child to understand. It is reasonable that toys might be removed if a child's misbehavior does not improve after one or two chances, but removal should not be the first action.

Gentle but firm guidance can improve behavior. It is also important to recognize that physical punishment drives a wedge of fear and resentment between parent and child. Reasonable limits may make the child angry at times but does not strain the parent/child relationship.

Parents with mental retardation need to learn that *all* children require limit setting in order to know what they may or may not do. The parents need to know that these limits must generally be based on:

1. The child's age
2. The child's capabilities (i.e., child development information)
3. The parent's needs (e.g., if a specific television show is very
   important to the parent, the child's need for attention
   must be met at other time periods)

It is important to note that children who live with clear
limits are happier and more secure than children who are never
able to predict how behaviors will be received by parents.

In setting limits, parents need to consider their child's day
so that appropriate limits can be set around such routines as
indoor and outdoor playtimes, bathtime, meals, bedtimes, and
naps. The professional parenting staff will need to be involved
as these decisions are made. Implementing and monitoring
limits will require intensive staff involvement over long periods
of time (see Figure 5.3).

---

**Safety and Security for the child, Sanity for the parents**

Limits must be set so that the child is kept:

**Safe**      2-year-olds cannot be trusted to stay on the sidewalk; some
            five-year-olds can, so the limit is:

    1.  Play in fenced yard (if available), or
    2.  Play on sidewalk only if Mother is along.

**Secure**    For a young child, security is based on having things happen
            in the same way every day and in having today's "No's" be
            tomorrow's "No's." If the child jumps on Mother's bed, that's
            a "No" yesterday, today, and tomorrow. Rules need to be
            consistent, so the limit is:

    1.  Jump on the floor.
    2.  No jumping on Mother's bed.

Limits on the child's behavior must also be based on what Mother and
Father can reasonably live with:

**Sanity**    Having the child use a quiet, indoor voice may be important to
            one parent but not to another. Though some of the limits set
            for the child may seem to be only for the parents' benefit this
            may not necessarily be the only benefit. Anything that helps
            the parents cope ultimately benefits the child.

---

Figure 5.3.   The three S's of limit setting.

# MODULE 2: THE CHILD'S BASIC NEEDS

## BACKGROUND

Most parents who have mental retardation will be able to list food, clothing, a place to live, and perhaps a caretaker as basic needs for children. It is much less likely that they will think of the needs their children will have in terms of emotional growth. To what extent can these parents learn to identify, let alone meet, these important needs? What can the parenting staff do to teach these important concepts?

It must first be recognized that few parents with mental retardation start out with adequate self-esteem. They have rarely experienced anything approaching adequate nurturance, love, or security. Thus, we must try to help parents with mental retardation provide for their children something that they may not have experienced in their own lives.

To begin, we try to teach the parents the importance of children's needs. We support and model and help wherever possible. It is, however, equally important to attempt to fill these basic human needs in the lives of parents. The extent to which a mother with mental retardation will be able to meet the needs of her children may well depend on the ability of the professional staff to nurture, accept, and give approval to her as she learns.

It will be necessary to teach and reteach the importance of meeting these basic needs in every possible way. Module 2 cannot consist of four, six, or eight sessions and come to an end. Sessions will need to be retaught at fixed intervals after the initially scheduled sessions. Most important will be a continued emphasis on these needs through all components of the center- and home-based aspects of the PLT program.

Home visits represent an especially good opportunity to provide parental feedback. Parents with mental retardation need to be given positive feedback for positive interactions. Interactions in which the parent might have performed better will also be noted. The style of this feedback will be as matter of fact as possible. The staff member will need to repeatedly express confidence that the parent will do better next time.

## GOALS AND OBJECTIVES

Goal:   Parents develop skills that help in addressing their children's basic needs

Objective 1.    The parent will communicate love verbally and through body language during daily routines, with parental progress documented by staff observation 3 out of 4 data collection days.

Objective 2.    The parent will give the child attention and verbal feedback when the child performs routine tasks or plays constructively, with parental progress documented by staff observation 3 out of 4 data collection days.

Objective 3.    The parent will provide the child opportunity for self-help skills as the child becomes more competent, with parental progress documented by staff observation 3 out of 4 data collection days.

Objective 4.    The parent will set specific limits on indoor and outdoor play to ensure child safety, with parental progress documented by staff observation 3 out of 4 data collection days.

## SAMPLE SESSION

This session will introduce parents to the basic emotional needs of children as human beings.

### Large Group Discussion

Children will be in playroom with caregivers. Group leader will have a chart with pictures that demonstrate the physical needs of children, such as clothing, shelter, food, and physical care (e.g., diapering). The leader will facilitate the discussion's progression starting from the obvious physical needs of children and moving to the equally important basic needs for good emotional health. The five basic emotional needs will be identified (see pp. 79–80). Parents will be allowed to ask questions or comment briefly. The leader will then divide the group into several smaller groups of no more than three family units and one staff member.

### Small Group Activity

Each group will discuss Need Number One and then try to think of specific ways to ensure that this need is being filled for their children. Each parent will then begin a picture book of the Five Basic Needs. For the first session each parent should complete several pages on Need Number One.

## Large Group Sharing

The groups will then reassemble to share the discoveries of the small groups. Allow each group to review some of their discussion points and demonstrate some of the pictures in their books. As these pictures are shared and as the discussion proceeds, some parents will begin to realize that these child needs are also adult needs. If not, the leader will need to point out how this is so and then proceed to demonstrate with examples showing that, whatever our age, all human beings have the same basic needs. Some of the needs may vary at different ages, but there indeed exist needs that *all* human beings share. The leader may end with the plan to work on Need Number Two in the next session and the reminder that all will look for opportunities to make Need Number One meaningful in the lives of their children each day.

Following are some verbatim responses given by a group of parents with mental retardation who had just been exposed to a brief explanation and one activity session related to the Five Basic Needs.

**Need Number One:** The need to be loved and accepted unconditionally

    Janet: "Touch 'em lots."
     Gail: "Treat all the same," (this mother had a 12-year-old girl and a 4-year-old boy).
  Barbara: "Tell the child you love them, praise them when they do right."

**Need Number Two:** The need for security, that is, to be safe and relatively free from threats

     Joe: "Keep the kids away from steps; use a gate; keep 'em away from stoves and poison stuff."
     Jan: "Gotta keep away from rat traps."
     Jim: "Keep a table in front of light sockets."
   Carole: "Watch those kids on bikes."

**Need Number Three:** The need to belong, to be a part of the group, and to feel identification and acceptance

   Carole: "Billy, him all I have; I say Billy, we family."
     Mary: "I love Jimmy."

**Need Number Four:** The need to be recognized, to gain approval, to feel significant and accepted for the way one functions

Carole:  "Billy, he helps take clothes to the basement."
Jan:  "Watch when her feed the doll."
Mary:  "Thank you; you help clean house!"

**Need Number Five:** The need to be independent, to take responsibility, and to make choices

Ginny:  "Buy cowboy boots."
Jan:  "Put shoes away."
Carole:  "Help clean room."

The above comments indicate that the parents responded with very concrete suggestions. This is precisely what could be expected. Further suggestions, role-playing, and picture activities all helped to deepen understanding and added to each parent's store of ideas. Home visits provided opportunities to point out occasions when parents were succeeding as well as times when different responses were needed.


## INFORMATION PARENTS NEED

Parents with mental retardation need to learn that all children (and all adults, too) can be emotionally healthy and happy only to the extent that the Five Basic Needs are being met. Explain that there is no special time of day when parents work on these needs. All the things parents do *with* and *for* their child all day long can help to meet these important needs. See the following examples:

1.  Give your child a quick hug as you walk past him to start cooking.
2.  Say to child, "No! You may not hit me! It's O.K. to be mad at me, and I love you *even* when you're mad, but you *may not* hit!"
3.  Say, "I like the way you put *all* the pieces of your toy back in the box. You are my good helper."
4.  "I *like* your picture. You used green, blue, yellow. You did it *all* by yourself!"
5.  "You are growing so fast! Look at all the things you can do!
    a.  You go potty all by yourself.
    b.  You can put on your own shoes.
    c.  You can take off your shirt.
    You can *really* do things!"

If the child is having his or her needs met most of the time, he or she is more likely to be a happy, secure, pleasant person to live with. He or she will not be happy all of the time, of course, nor will he or she always be obedient. In general, however, the child's problems will be fewer, as will the parents'.

## RESOURCES AND ADDITIONAL ACTIVITIES

All of the Five Basic Needs can be presented as was Need Number One. Picture book pages on each need will be made as each one is highlighted. Throughout the period of time each parent is involved in the parenting course, basic needs should be highlighted and referred to whenever possible. The modeling done by staff members throughout the program will provide the best opportunity to highlight and give due importance to the basic needs.

# MODULE 3: PARENT/CHILD INTERACTION

## BACKGROUND

The concept of appropriate supervision of child play in either parent-involved or parent-supervised play may be completely foreign to a mother or father with mental retardation. The problem is compounded when there is more than one child to be considered. The factors listed below seem to affect parent performance during parent-involved and parent-supervised playtimes.

1. Parents who have been monitored by a Division of Family Services (DFS) housekeeper are often warned that a dirty house will "get them into trouble and cause them to lose their children." Limited understanding may cause the parent to equate messy housekeeping with the normal clutter generated by children at play. The child may then be allowed only one toy at a time for hours, with the parent becoming angry or frustrated when "her don't even play with it." One couple kept their 18-month-old boy in his crib with a small push toy. The floor remained uncluttered and met DFS standards for keeping the child in the home, while the child's motor skills lagged.

2. Some mothers with mental retardation, convinced of the importance of play, may have a number of multipart toys

available with the pieces all dumped together. If the child sifts through this toy junk pile, the parent feels play is going well.

3.   Keeping children safe while at play is a responsibility requiring judgment and a level of alertness that is often difficult for any parents, especially those who have mental retardation, to sustain. Even a mother who knows to store medicines and other dangerous substances appropriately out of the children's reach may be oblivious to the potential dangers inherent in some toys. A mother who provides a toddler with a toy containing small pieces that can be swallowed is not demonstrating her lack of concern for her child; rather she is exhibiting her inability to judge age appropriateness. To make matters more complicated, a young child playing with age-appropriate toys still requires supervision. Pieces can break off, and young children sometime end up using appropriate toys in potentially dangerous ways. Consider the difficulty that both toy manufacturers and parents who do not have mental disabilities have in determining safety and age appropriateness.

4.   It is difficult for adults with mental retardation to focus on more than one thing at a time. The parent may become so completely involved in what he or she is doing (e.g., washing dishes, hanging clothes) that he or she forgets to monitor the play of the children. As a group, adults with mental retardation are not good at keeping an eye and ear tuned to the child while otherwise occupied. Furthermore, if such a parent does stop to give the child help, he or she may become so engrossed in the child's activity that, for example, the sink overflows onto the floor.

5.   Despite obvious good intentions to play with their children or monitor the children's play, parents with mental retardation may get caught up in their own interests. For example, the child may be forgotten as Mother watches her favorite television show.

6.   In many ways a parent with mental retardation is childlike. The parent may be so hungry for fun that he or she takes over while the child becomes a frustrated or passive onlooker as the parent plays with the toys.

It is easy for professionals to feel discouraged, even overwhelmed, in the face of these difficulties. It helps to remind oneself of the fact that this parent has probably received little appreciation, stimulation, or even interest in his or her own life. Again, staff must continue to be "parents" to these parents while guiding them to do a better job with their own children.

## GOALS AND OBJECTIVES

Goal I.   Parents develop skills in direct play with their children.

Objective 1.   Mother/Father will communicate with child both verbally and nonverbally during play time.

Objective 2.   Mother/Father will set necessary safety limits in the use of toys.

Objective 3.   Mother/Father will play with child without taking over play as child watches.

Objective 4.   Mother/Father will set a tone of fun while playing with child.

(Note: Percentage of achievement for each objective should be decided on an individual basis. Factors to be considered include: 1) current level of function, 2) IQ, and 3) motivation.)

Goal II.   The parent supervises child's play activities while going about his or her work.

Objective 1.   Parent will check on child frequently if child is playing out of sight (at a time interval appropriate to the child's age, activity).

Objective 2.   Parent will provide fresh toys or offer new ideas for play as child tires of current activity.

Objective 3.   Parent will give the child quick hugs and touches while going about his or her work.

Objective 4.   Parent will stop and provide snacks, tender loving care, or other attention as needed.

Figure 5.4 shows a test to be administered to parents before and, again, after Module 3.

## SAMPLE SESSION I: PARENT-INVOLVED PLAY

This component of Module 3 is best worked on initially in the center-based portion of the program. Later it will be important to help parents schedule specific playtimes at home. While the direct play experience for each parent is individualized, the parents benefit from and enjoy the group experiences. Moreover, these group activities facilitate a sense of belonging with-

| | | | | |
|---|---|---|---|---|
| 1. | Toys shoud be kept out of the child's reach. | T | F | Don't Know |
| 2. | The child should have no more than one toy at a time. | T | F | Don't Know |
| 3. | If the child is playing with his or her toys, parent can watch TV or do housework without frequent checking. | T | F | Don't Know |
| 4. | Babies too young to hold toys do not need a playtime with parent. | T | F | Don't Know |
| 5. | Toys bought at stores are safe and can be used by your child at any time. | T | F | Don't Know |
| 6. | Toys are *never* dangerous. | T | F | Don't Know |
| 7. | Toys should be kept on a low shelf or in a corner on the floor so that the child can choose what he or she wants. | T | F | Don't Know |
| 8. | If you know your child is playing with a safe toy you do not need to watch him or her. | T | F | Don't Know |
| 9. | The child should have toys only when Mother or Father can play with him or her. | T | F | Don't Know |
| 10. | Babies from birth to 2 years old should not be allowed to put things in their mouths. | T | F | Don't Know |
| 11. | Only store-bought toys will help the child learn. | T | F | Don't Know |
| 12. | Only babies and little children need playtime with Mother and Father. 3- and 4-year-olds should play by themselves or with friends. | T | F | Don't Know |
| 13. | If your child has a toy to play with and you are busy, the child should not be allowed to bother you. | T | F | Don't Know |
| 14. | The child should have toys *only* when Mother and Father can play with him or her. | T | F | Don't Know |
| 15. | Children 2, 3, and 4 years old should not be allowed to fight about toys. They are old enough to share all the time. | T | F | Don't Know |
| 16. | Young children enjoy games like (as Mother or Father holds toy dog) "The doggie's gonna get you!" | T | F | Don't Know |
| 17. | Games like "The doggie's gonna get you" or "Here comes the monster" are scary. | T | F | Don't Know |

Figure 5.4.    Pretest/Posttest for Module 3: Parent/Child Interaction.

in the group in addition to both staff teaching and client learning. In order to best encourage play activities with the high-risk children of parents with mental retardation, it is first important that the children be developmentally assessed. One can use an instrument such as the Brigance Diagnostic Inventory of Early Development (Brigance, 1978) to yield developmental age levels that can be used to set appropriate play goals. A poster board (folded in half so it will stand) can be constructed for each child, with several appropriate activities listed. Since many of the adult clients with mental retardation are illiterate, activities can be represented by stick figures or simple outline drawings. Plan to use continued parent-child play activities (such as the sample initial session included) as a part of all future sessions so that parents have a chance to practice direct play with their children.

### Large Group Discussion

*Introduction*   The group leader prepares the group for a demonstration of parent-child playtime and, later, practice time. The parents are asked to watch the demonstration and try to remember what the parent says and does, and what the child says and does.

*Demonstration*   The staff leader acts as Mother with a child, Gina, age 22 months.

Materials needed:   Large poster board indicating Gina's activities

Toy for one of the activities (e.g., a bucket containing five or six small items)

Mother: "Let's sit here, Gina." Mother places bucket with assorted small items on floor between herself and the child. As Gina touches bucket, "Yes, Gina! Bucket!" As Gina dumps items on floor, "Lots of things! You dumped them *all* out! Look, Gina, I'm putting a yellow comb in the bucket." Gina picks up small car and throws it in the bucket. Then Mother hugs Gina and says, "Hey! You put the car in the bucket. Good! I see a little doll! Can you find the doll, Gina?" Gina tentatively picks up doll and holds it up to Mother. Mother: "Good! (as she claps for Gina). Put the doll in the bucket." Gina does so. Demonstration continues for 2 or 3 minutes more.

### Large Group Sharing

The group leader begins, "All right, let's talk about what we saw." The leader writes observations made by the parents on the board or chart; comments may be similar to the following:

1.  "Mother told Gina what she was doing: 'You dumped everything out.'"
2.  "Mother watched Gina all of the time."
3.  "Mother told Gina, 'Good.'"
4.  "Mother had fun too!"

After all the parents have had an opportunity to share observations and ask questions, the staff leader will sum up by saying, for example, "Good watching, Moms! We saw a lot in a few minutes, didn't we? Let's look at the things we listed and see how we can use some of these ideas when we play with our own children." Reread the list, commenting and accepting more ideas. Using observations, the leader will try to bring out the following guidelines for playtime:

1.  Make the play fun.
2.  Encourage the child to explore and manipulate the toy. Say, "Turn it another way. What happened?"
3.  Describe what the child is doing. Say, "Tim is putting *all* the toys in the box."
4.  Help the child feel good about herself or himself with hugs, clapping, and words. Say, "Hey, you did it!"
5.  Keep the play safe. "Uh, oh! That piece broke off! Broken pieces go in the trashcan, not in your mouth. Let's go do it together!"
6.  Give help when needed. Say, "I see you're stuck. Try turning it another way."
7.  Give and ask for lots of eye contact. (Note:  These guidelines will be followed by staff from day one, but parents will learn slowly. Remember to give positive reinforcement for *every* gain.)

### Parent-Child Playtime Practice Session (15 Minutes)

Leader: "Now each of you can try it with your children." No more than four parents and their children are assigned to one parent aide. Parents and children are given baskets of toys and Plan Cards. As parent and child units begin to work, parent aides move among them facilitating play, modeling, and giving positive feedback wherever possible. At the end of the practice period, the children return to the playroom with their caretakers.

## Small Group Activity

Each group of four family units and one parent aide meets to discuss what happened, to describe what was good and what could have been better. Again, the parent aide gives as much positive reinforcement as possible. It is essential that every parent receive some positive comments. The "sandwich principle" applies here:

The bottom slice of bread: Verbal recognition of something well done

The filling: Discussion of some things that might be tried differently another time

The top slice of bread: Another positive verbal recognition

## Large Group Sharing

Leader: "Everyone worked hard. I think we all deserve a big hand." All clap.

## SAMPLE SESSION II: PARENT-SUPERVISED PLAY

Every home visit you make, regardless of the primary purpose (e.g. budgeting, safety, living skills), will provide opportunities to work on supervising child play. Your awareness of what the children are doing and your responses to them will be perhaps the best way to teach your client how important it is to respond to the children even while going about household chores. Over time, you will want to help each parent to:

1.  Find convenient storage places for toys
2.  Set reasonable limits for play
3.  Plan ways to enrich child play by conversation or adding toys at appropriate times

## INFORMATION PARENTS NEED

When you play with your child:

1.  You are helping him or her learn.
2.  You are building a warm, close, loving relationship with your child.

3.  You are helping your child feel good about himself or her-self; you are giving him or her important messages such as:
    A.  I like you.
    B.  Things that are important to you are important to me, too.
    C.  You are important to me.
    D.  It's fun to be together.

When your child has special times with you:

1.  He or she can more easily accept times when you cannot stop and play.
2.  The child develops play skills he or she can use when you are not available.

## ACTIVITIES AND RESOURCES

Made-up songs to familiar tunes can be used at group singing times to reinforce the importance of parents paying attention to their children. An example follows:

Tune:   "Flies in the Buttermilk"

> Baby's crying, wah, wah, wah.
> What does Baby need?
> Maybe Baby's wet, wet, wet.
> We will look and see.

> No, Baby's dry!
> Baby's crying, wah, wah, wah.
> What does Baby need?
> Maybe baby's too hot, too cold?
> We will look and see.

> No, Baby's dressed just about right.
> Baby's crying, wah, wah, wah.
> What does Baby need?
> Maybe Baby wants to be held?
> We will pick her up.

# MODULE 4: PERSONAL AND CHILD HYGIENE

## BACKGROUND

Few individuals with mental retardation now reaching adulthood have had the benefit of lifelong programming services. Many have had some special education classes or training in self-help skills, but few will have received training tailored to their individual needs throughout the life span. Today preschoolers who have mental retardation are already establishing good self-help habits. Moreover, children with mental retardation are now eligible for continuing special education geared to their individual needs through age 21. Personal hygiene and grooming habits that will be second nature when these preschoolers reach adulthood were not taught in the past and have not been incorporated into the daily routine of many of today's young adults with mental retardation.

This means that parents who have mental retardation must be educated to establish good personal hygiene habits for themselves as well as their children. Learning to care for one's self while simultaneously becoming responsible for children is a formidable task. Establishing these new habits can be made even more difficult in many cases because of inadequate facilities in the client's home. If hot water is not available, taking a bath may involve pouring water into an old-fashioned wash tub. Washing and drying clothes may involve leaning over a bathtub full of clothes and then hanging clothes on lines crisscrossing the bedroom, or may necessitate dragging heavy laundry bags several blocks to a laundromat. It is not unusual to find mountains of dirty clothes and a bag of clean thrift shop purchases sitting side by side in many homes with parents who have mental retardation. Nothing can be assumed. One mother washed the family's clothes in an old-style wringer washer, using huge amounts of detergent. The clothes were not rinsed, but immediately hung on lines on the open porch in both summer and winter. Both children and adults had pruritis, and one infant's skin exhibited erythematous wheals. In the absence of home visits, the dermatologic etiology would have remained unknown. Another mother with mental retardation was taught by her mother, who also had a mental disability, how to wash clothes in a wringer-type washer that had been in the back yard for several years. Neither had thought to scrub the tub, so the clothes were dirtier after the wash than before.

As in many aspects of their lives, these parents' management of personal and child hygiene may be inconsistent. One mother kept her 3-year-old immaculate, yet she herself had greasy hair and a distinctly unpleasant odor. One father appeared neat and clean, while his 2-year-old smelled of urine, and the child's clothes were obviously mud-splattered and dirty. Some parents with mental retardation wear clean clothing over dirty bodies, and others wear dirty clothes on clean bodies. Even after the parent has learned what must be done, there may remain ongoing problems. Setting a schedule for personal hygiene and remembering to keep to the schedule pose continuing difficulties. The token economy has proved especially helpful in establishing better hygiene habits. Purchasing clothing and attractively packaged personal care products in the program's store serve as incentives and help the parents take pride in their own and their children's appearance. Most important, the professional staff must remain supportive as new habits are being established. This area of learning takes more time and repetition than almost any other. It must be kept in mind that while two steps forward and one step backward is apt to be the pattern, growth *is* nevertheless taking place.


## GOALS AND OBJECTIVES

Goal I.   Parents will practice necessary personal hygiene habits on a regular basis.
   Objective 1.   The parent will take a bath daily.
   Objective 2.   The parent will wash his or her hair at least 3 times a week.
   Objective 3.   The parent will wear clean clothing.
   Objective 4.   The parent will brush his or her teeth 2–3 times a day.

Goal II.   The parent will see that his or her children are cared for.
   Objective 1.   Children will be given a bath daily.
   Objective 2.   Children's hair will be washed at least 3 times a week.
   Objective 3.   Children will wear clean clothing.
   Objective 4.   Children will brush their teeth 3 times a day. (Younger children will be helped by parents.)
   (Note:   Parents will be encouraged to teach the child to take as much responsibility for self-help routines as possible.)

Figures 5.5 and 5.6 show tests to be administered to parents before and, again, after Module 4.

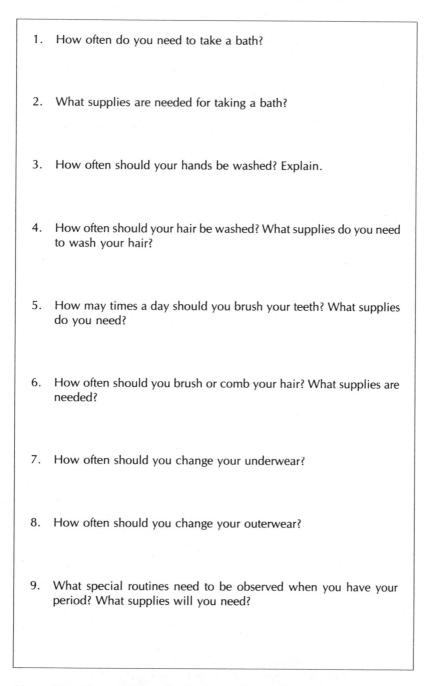

1. How often do you need to take a bath?

2. What supplies are needed for taking a bath?

3. How often should your hands be washed? Explain.

4. How often should your hair be washed? What supplies do you need to wash your hair?

5. How may times a day should you brush your teeth? What supplies do you need?

6. How often should you brush or comb your hair? What supplies are needed?

7. How often should you change your underwear?

8. How often should you change your outerwear?

9. What special routines need to be observed when you have your period? What supplies will you need?

Figure 5.5.    Pretest/Posttest for Module 4: Personal Hygiene.

1.  Can some clothing be worn more than once? Explain.

2.  How are shoes cared for? Supplies needed?

3.  How do you know which clothes can be washed and which must be dry-cleaned?

4.  What clothing needs to be ironed?

5.  What must be done to keep clothes in good repair?

Figure 5.6.   Pretest/Posttest for Module 4: Clothing.

**SAMPLE SESSION**

In this session, the parents will be guided to think about and plan how to fit necessary health and personal hygiene habits into the day's schedule.

**Large Group Discussion**

The group leader will have ready pictures (easily found in magazines) of adults and children brushing teeth, bathing, and so forth, and a large felt board to put them on. The leader may begin, "Today we're going to plan how we can get bathing, brushing teeth, and other important things done every day. It's hard and takes a great deal of time, but I *know* you can do it! Each of you has pictures of some of the health habits we all have to work into our busy day. As we put the pictures up on the board, we'll talk about each one."

The leader may then ask each parent in turn to put a picture on the flannel board. As each picture goes up, the leader guides the group to look thoughtfully at it. The group will be encouraged to talk about each habit shown in the pictures and decide the time or times each day the activity should be done.

*Example 1*   One mother puts up pictures of an adult and child brushing their teeth. The leader guides the group to decide when and how many times a day this task is necessary. The group also discusses why this habit is important to good health.

*Example 2*   A father puts up a picture of a child washing her hands as the mother stands by giving encouragement. The leader guides the group in discussing when and under what circumstances children should wash their hands.

When the activity is completed or the leader sees attention beginning to wane, the large group is divided into smaller groups. No more than three family units should be included in each group with one staff member as leader.

### Small Group Activity

The leader will guide each family to plan sufficient time for each health routine for every family member.

### Large Group Sharing

The leader will reconvene the large group and take a few minutes for each group or family to share their specific plans. Motivating the parents by reassuring each one that you *know* they will succeed is essential. As progress is monitored over the next days and weeks, reinforce every honest effort. If you continually recall how difficult these efforts are for many of these parents, you will find that reinforcing "mole hills" while waiting for "mountains" will become a great deal easier.

## INFORMATION PARENTS NEED

In every possible way (e.g., charts, stories, conversation, modeling) the parents must become aware of the importance of keeping themselves and their children clean. The parents need to know that keeping themselves and their children clean means clean bodies, clean hair, clean teeth, and clean clothing.

They need to know that keeping a family clean and keeping clothing clean *does* mean time and work. They need to know that cleanliness is important if they are to be accepted by others. As one mother said of a valued friend, "Her stays longer I don't smell!" Some parents who cannot be reached in terms of personal pride or socialization, care very much what others think about their babies. "My baby had *two* baths today—he's beautiful."

While good health is an adequate motivator for other people, it may not mean a great deal to some adults who have mental retardation, at least not in general. Specific cause and effect relationships may have a greater impact. For example, a mother worn out with frequent clinic appointments for diaper rash in a crying, fussy baby is more apt to recognize the health component of clean diapers, frequent changes, and a clean baby.

As the parents develop the necessary health habits, they need to know *you* are proud of them. Most of all, they need to be proud of themselves. They need to feel that all the work and time translate into "I'm a *good* parent!"

## ACTIVITIES AND RESOURCES

After discussing the need to wash hands, let parents work on individual or group charts, gluing magazine pictures on to poster board to illustrate various activities that require hand-washing beforehand or afterward.

Make up a song to a familiar tune to reinforce the importance of parents keeping their children clean:

> This is the way we wash our hands,
> wash our hands,
> wash our hands.

> This is the way we wash our hands
> Before we cook the meat,
> Before we set the table,
> Before we slice tomatoes,
> Before we eat our lunch.

> This is the way we wash our hands
> After bathroom time,
> After changing diapers,
> After mopping floors,
> After doing housework.

This and similar songs can be used at group singing times without additional comments.

Bathing infants and young children can be good parent-child interaction times. Each body part can be named as it is being washed. Mother can also sing about the body parts. Use traditional melody or simply chant:

> Now we wash Annie's nose;
> Now we wash Annie's nose;
> Now we wash Annie's nose,
>     And it's all clean!

> How many toes does Bryan have?
> How many toes does Bryan have?
>     Bryan has ten toes.
>     Let's wash them all!

Each parent can make a picture book of health habits using magazine pictures of family members brushing teeth, bathing, and so forth. Parenting staff will have opportunities to talk about good habits while the book is in progress. The picture book can be taken home, and parents can teach their children (and themselves) as it is used.

# MODULE 5:
# DAILY ROUTINES TO MEET FAMILY NEEDS

## BACKGROUND

For many families headed by an adult with mental retardation, a daily schedule as people generally understand one is virtually nonexistent. Many of these families have no particular mealtimes. Parents and children alike eat or are fed when they are hungry and food is available. Bedtime for the children may come "whenever they fall asleep." This may happen in front of the television, in the crib where they have spent most of the day, or anywhere else in the house. Bedtime for parents may be whenever they "feel" like retiring, and that may be after children are put to bed, or it may occur while preschoolers are still wandering around. The same attitude may be taken for getting up from bed. The safety hazards for unsupervised young children are considerable. Since many adults with mental retardation have little, if any, concept of time, this state of affairs is not surprising.

The disorganization in which these families live is difficult to change, but change it must if adequate child care is to take place. Research supports the clinical impression of child development professionals that the lack of a predictable routine contributes to insecurity in young children. Clearly, lack of schedule leads to missed medical appointments, unwashed clothes, unprepared meals, and neglected children.

Helping even motivated parents (and many are unmotivated) establish a schedule is a difficult task. The following must be established:

1.  A way to tell time (e.g., giving evening medicine after a particular television show)
2.  The clear priority of constant child supervision regardless of other task involvement
3.  A schedule of all necessary personal routines for each and every family member
4.  Most important, commitment by each parent to the necessity of keeping the routine

With our clients, the token economy strategy has been extremely helpful to establish habits and routines. The token economy provided external motivation until internal motivation could be developed.

## GOALS AND OBJECTIVES

Parents develop a family schedule to meet basic needs.

Objective 1.  To formulate a schedule for weekly housecleaning, kept with 90% accuracy.

Objective 2.  To formulate a schedule to allow for daily and weekly health routines, kept with 90% accuracy.

Objective 3.  To formulate a schedule to allow for the monitoring of child safety during daily routines, kept with 90% accuracy.

Objective 4.  To formulate a schedule allowing for at least one activity per child per day, kept with 90% accuracy.

## SAMPLE SESSION

Daily routines for morning and evening will be run through.

### Large Group Discussion

Group leader: "Today we're going to try to put together many of the things we've been learning (leader points to health habits charts). Remember, we've practiced all the health routines, and we've talked about and practiced playing with our children (leader points to play charts and toy shelves). We know the house must be cleaned and shopping done, too. We know *all* these things must be done, but sometimes the day seems too short. We've talked about all this before, but as we get ready to plan our morning and evening schedules in greater detail, would some of you help start our thinking by sharing some of the problems you've had?" Answers may include: "Just remembering," "Getting up that early," "Having time," "I'm too tired," "Child won't help," "No time left to watch TV." Leader: "Yes, all these problems are very real. We're going to try to make it a little easier. Another day, we'll work on a full-day schedule and talk about a way to keep the house clean and get the shopping done. We think each family needs a schedule planned especially for it. We're going to break into small groups and get started. Everyone ready?" (The group is divided into smaller groups with no more than two family units to a staff member.)

## Small Group Activity

The staff leader will help each family construct a schedule considering the following variables:

1. Number of adults in home
2. Number of children in home
3. Ages of children in home
4. Sleep needs of each child
5. Each child's needs for time alone with Mother and Father
6. Mother's and Father's need for time alone together

Leader: "Today we're going to work on those two really busy times—time to get up and time to go to bed. We're going to try to find ways to get everything done and give attention to our children, too." A morning schedule might look like Figure 5.7. Getting the bare bones of the schedule outlined is a necessary first step, but the parents will need additional reminders of the importance of cuddling, talking to, and listening to their children as these routines are carried out. Naturally, rising times will vary, based on other family commitments. An evening schedule might look like Figure 5.8. Obviously, the schedule will differ in one-parent homes. In two-parent homes, Mother and Father will have time alone with different children on different days.

**Family: Mother, 3¹/₂-month-old Max, 2-year-old Irene**

6:00 a.m.: Mother wakens, washes and dresses self, and gets bottle and breakfast ready for children.

6:30 a.m.: Mother gets Max from crib, changes diaper and other clothes if necessary; gives Max bottle, cereal, and fruit; places Max in infant seat, where he can watch as Mother changes crib sheets.

7:00 a.m.: Mother bathes Max, dresses him in clean clothes, and puts him down for a nap. Mother gets 2-year-old Irene up, takes wet bedding off bed. If bed is wet, Irene is bathed and dressed in clean, dry clothes.

7:15 a.m.: Mother sets out breakfast for herself and Irene.

Figure 5.7.   Morning schedule.

**Family: Father, Mother, 6-month-old Sherry, 2-year-old Liz, 3-year-old Ben**

6:45 p.m.: 6-month-old Sherry's bath time and special time with Father. Father bathes and dresses Sherry for bed. Plays with and cuddles her. Holds her for her bottle. Mother watches Liz and Ben as they play or watch television.

7:30 p.m.: Mother and Father put Sherry to bed with a kiss.

7:30 p.m.: 2-year-old Liz's bath time and special time with Mother. Mother bathes Liz and dresses her for bed. Afterwards, Mother reads and sings to Liz as they cuddle in rocking chair. Father watches Ben as he plays, and listens for Sherry.

8:15 p.m.: Liz goes to bed. Mother and Father tuck her in with a goodnight kiss.

8:15 p.m.: Ben's bath time and special time with Father. Father bathes Ben and dresses him for bed. After the bath, Father reads to Ben as they cuddle. Mother listens for Sherry and Liz and straightens up bathroom, puts clothes in hamper, and so forth.

9:00 p.m.: Bedtime for Ben. Mother and Father tuck him in with kiss. Mother and Father have time together.

10:00 p.m.: Mother bathes and prepares for bed.

10:30 p.m.: Father bathes and prepares for bed.

11:00 p.m.: Mother and Father go to bed.

Figure 5.8.   Evening schedule.

## Large Group Sharing

After reconvening the large group, the leader will again highlight the importance of the daily routine, give positive feedback to the parents, and make plans with them for in-home follow-up of the completed individual schedule or, if this is incomplete, plan to continue work on it during the next session. Allow time for the parents to comment on or question the schedules worked out to this point. Accept their concerns and assure them of continued support.

## INFORMATION PARENTS NEED

*All* families, big and small, rich or poor, busy or not, must find time to:

1. Keep their homes clean
2. Follow health routines
3. Be aware of and supervise their children's safety
4. Spend time alone with each child

When there exists a daily and weekly plan that includes all these important components, it is easier not to forget one or more of them. When the weekly plan is followed (even though it will not always work perfectly), things get done and parents have more time for each other and themselves.

## ACTIVITIES AND RESOURCES

Picture charts of homemaking tasks (e.g., sweeping, dusting, mopping) can be used to initiate discussion.

Parents can make their own books (using magazine pictures) to remind them of the daily tasks that must be accomplished.

Role-playing of various daily routines can be done, especially for routines that include interaction with other family members.

Make large calendars and help the parents mark medical appointments in ways they can understand.

Provide small purse-size calendars also marked with appointments.

# MODULE 6: TIME CONCEPTS

## BACKGROUND

During the course of the program, numerous situations occurred that demonstrated the lack of time concept among our clients. Following are examples of this problem:

One day an appointment for a potential new client had been scheduled for 9:30 a.m. (at the client's request). The appointed time came and went. At 10:30, the client called and told us that she was getting ready to come for her appointment. Upon being questioned, she revealed that she had no idea that she was late.

Another client came to the center wearing a new digital watch. He was very proud of the watch, so to allow him a chance to impress the others, a staff member asked him how long it was until lunch at 11:30. The client repeatedly told us in a variety of ways that it was 10:45 but was not able to estimate the amount of time until lunch.

Another client was consistently unreliable about telling us when her children's clinic appointments were scheduled. When the day of an appointment arrived, one of two things happened: if she was at our center, we would have to remind her to go to her appointment; if she was not at the center, we would inevitably get a call from the clinic telling us that the appointment had not been kept. The client had every intention of keeping the appointments; she simply did not know how to tell time.

We live in a time-oriented society, full of appointments and schedules. Persons who have mental retardation are more subject to difficulties with time concepts than many other people. Appointments are sent in letter form to these persons, who are largely illiterate, telling them when to appear at clinics, for hearings, and to complete applications. In addition many of our clients were simply below the cognitive level necessary for adequate comprehension of time concepts. These clients needed compensatory systems such as receiving many reminder telephone calls.

## GOALS AND OBJECTIVES

Goal:   Parents improve time concepts.
        Objective 1.   To tell time to the nearest ½ hour with 90% accuracy
        Objective 2.   To match day of the week and date on a calendar with 90% accuracy.

## SAMPLE SESSION

### Large Group Discussion

Group leaders will have an enlarged calendar with the name of the month written next to each day of the month, for example, December 2. The concept of December 2, also represented as 12-2, will be discussed. Parents will be instructed to find the date and then identify the corresponding day of the week. Each parent will be given a small pocket calendar book and instructions to write all appointments and telephone numbers in it. The leader will then divide the group into smaller groups of no more than three family units and one staff member.

### Small Group Activity

Each small group will list the birthdays of the parents and their children. They will find the appropriate day of the week and date on the calendar and write down the day of the week and date of the birthday for the calendar year in their calendar books.

### Large Group Sharing

The group will then reassemble for a generalization activity. Each parent will be given a card with an upcoming holiday (month and day) on it. The parent will have to find the corresponding day of the week and date on the calendar and then tell the group which holiday it is and on what day of the week the holiday will be celebrated. Each member of the group will record the holiday in his or her pocket calendar.

## INFORMATION PARENTS NEED

Parents need to know that all of us occasionally forget appointments. The appropriate thing to do when we forget is to immediately call the person with whom we have the appointment in order to apologize and then make another appointment.

## RESOURCES AND ACTIVITIES

Parents should keep the following available:

1. Time and temperature telephone numbers
2. Radios
3. Digital clocks

# MODULE 7: MEDICAL CARE

## BACKGROUND

Obtaining medical care can be a confusing and frustrating process for the general population. The feelings of confusion and frustration are intensified for persons with mental retardation. The process is more complicated for such persons in three basic areas: degree of need, availability of medical services, and medical limitations.

It is well documented that persons with mental retardation and their children are at high risk for hereditary and acquired medical conditions. This population generally has a greater need for medical care. Among our clients it was discovered that all of the adults needed emergency dental care and well over 90% had unidentified and/or untreated hearing and visual impairments. Few, if any, of the women had received any gynecological care since they left the hospital following the birth of their children.

Availability of medical services to this population is limited. Lack of funding prevented most from having an identifiable primary care physician. Those not on public aid rarely saw physicians or dentists at all. Those who received public aid often misused the local emergency rooms as primary care providers. These practices made follow-up practically impossible for a group of people for whom follow-up is a vital part of any medical care.

Cognitive limitations and lack of confidence also interfered with obtaining medical care. Pretesting scores suggested difficulty understanding directions, remembering and scheduling appointments, recognizing and describing symptoms, and properly administering medication. Most disturbing was the fact that almost all of our clients did not question absurd recommendations given out during role-playing situations. Visits with parents to local clinics by members of our staff suggested a serious need for additional training of the medical community in dealing more effectively with persons who have mental retardation. Generally, medical professionals either ignored mentally retarded parents and talked with staff members accompanying them or talked with mentally retarded parents in ways that they could not understand. Some adults who were illiterate were given only written instructions, with no additional verbal explanation.

It is obvious that Module 7 cannot offer solutions for all of these problems. It is hoped that this module will help adults who have mental retardation to be more capable, independent, and confident at using medical services.

## GOALS AND OBJECTIVES

Goal.   Parents improve their ability to obtain medical care independently.

Objective 1.  To complete standard medical intake sheet requesting identifying information, with 90% accuracy

Objective 2.  To describe symptoms as measured by teacher observation during role-playing situations, with 90% accuracy

Objective 3.  To respond to questions concerning symptoms, measured by teacher observation during a role-playing situation, with 90% accuracy

Objective 4.  To demonstrate understanding of medical recommendations, as measured by teacher observation during a role-playing situation, with 90% accuracy

Objective 5.  To be able to identify a drug name from a prescription label, with 90% accuracy

Objective 6.  To interpret warning labels on prescription bottles, with 90% accuracy

Objective 7.  To verbally relate drug dosage and administration, with 90% accuracy

Objective 8.  To keep drugs in a safe place, as measured by home visit and personal report, with 90% accuracy

## SAMPLE SESSION

This session deals with enabling parents to interpret warning labels on prescription bottles with 90% accuracy.

### Large Group Discussion

The group leader will have a chart with enlargements of standard warning labels found on prescription bottles. The leader will discuss what each label means and why the label is important. Consequences of *not* knowing what the label means will be discussed. Questions and comments will be encouraged. The leader will then divide the group into smaller groups of no more than three family units and one staff member.

### Small Group Activity

Each small group will have sample prescription bottles with warning labels. They will practice interpreting the label and discuss what course of action (if any) to take based on the meaning of the label.

### Large Group Sharing

The groups will then reassemble for a generalization activity. Each parent will be given a bingo-type card with warning labels on it. The group leader will call out warning labels and the activity will proceed as a bingo game would.

### INFORMATION PARENTS NEED

Parents with mental retardation need to know that other people also find the medical process confusing and that *all* of us need to ask questions. They need to understand that medical personnel cannot answer questions that are not asked of them and that there is no such thing as a dumb question. This last concern reflects something that persons who have mental retardation are acutely sensitive about.

### RESOURCES AND ACTIVITIES

Parents should keep the following available:

1. Poison control telephone number
2. Hospital pharmacy telephone number
3. Hospital social worker telephone number

# MODULE 8: MAKING TOYS

### BACKGROUND

The majority of parents who have mental retardation live near or below poverty level. Seldom are there dollars that can be spared for anything other than basic needs. Sadly, these same people are perfect targets for media hype and are often led to spend money for basic needs on "TV super toys." This happens because:

1. The *parents* are easily influenced by television toy commercials.
2. Parents who have mental retardation may equate being good parents with giving things. (In this they are not alone.)
3. These parents want others to *see* they are good parents.
4. These parents have no way to judge the appropriateness of a given toy.
5. These parents have spent many years doing what they were told, and television is a good "teller."

In Module 8, we give the parents an opportunity to make inexpensive toys for their children. They will learn to see that an appropriate toy need not be an expensive toy. They will also derive satisfaction from discovering that they can provide for their children's needs in ways they had not thought about before. It is likely, too, that the parents will enjoy exercising their own creativity as well as appreciating the finished product. We have found toy making to be a high-interest activity for our clients. One problem, however, seems inherent to the activity. Some parents want to rush and make everything. It is important that parents be guided to work slowly and carefully. Close supervision and appropriate feedback can avoid the parents ending up with everything and nothing.

## GOALS AND OBJECTIVES

Goal I.  Parents make low-cost toys from available materials.

   Objective 1.  Parent will follow visual directions to make toys.

   Objective 2.  Parent will collect appropriate materials for toys.

Goal II.  Parents make safe toys.

   Objective 1.  Parent will be able to say if toy has sharp edges.

   Objective 2.  Parent will be able to say if toy has pieces that are *too* small.

Goal III.  Parents make toys that meet the developmental needs of the child.

Objective 1.   Parent will make toys that are developmentally appropriate for his or her children.

Objective 2.   Parent will be able to introduce finished toy to child and appropriately supervise play.

## SAMPLE SESSION

### Large Group Discussion

The group leader will talk to the group about the importance of providing appropriate toys for children. The leader will invite the group to think about the kinds of toys children enjoy.

Opportunity will be provided to look at store-bought and homemade toys that fill the same child needs (e.g., commercial rhythm toys and homemade rhythm toys, commercial pull toys and homemade pull toys). Using a prepared chart, the leader will then discuss the importance of toy safety. When the discussion is over, the leader will assign parents to smaller groups of no more than three family units and one staff member. Each group of parents should have children of approximately the same developmental age, so that the group members can choose and make similar toys.

### Small Group Activity

The parent aide leading each small group will discuss the appropriate needs of the children in the group. Several suggested toy projects will be discussed. Parents will make their choice, gather materials, and begin work. Parent aides may need to give more help as the parents begin work. It is important that the parents feel successful. Necessary help will be given, but most of that help should not include actual work on the project. Parent aides will, of course, give as much positive feedback as possible. For example:

"Mae, I like the way your nesting toy is looking! Your Joe is really ready for that toy. I can imagine how happy he'll be when he plays with it."

"Making that long train is going to be quite a job, Ella! You've certainly made a good start."

"I see you've decided to make musical toys, Jim. You and Annie will really have fun together!"

"How carefully you've cut those circles and squares for your put and take toy, Marilyn! Good for you!"

At the end of the work period, time should be taken for parents to clean their work area and put away the materials for the next work time. Before rejoining the large group, each small group should make plans for finishing their in-progress projects.

## Large Group Activity

The leader will ask each small group to share briefly. Again, positive feedback for the work being done is given liberally. It is particularly important to tie the positive reinforcement to the value the completed toys will have for the children.

## INFORMATION PARENTS NEED

### Choosing Toys

1. The toy must fit the child's developmental age and need.
2. The toy must be safe:
   A. No sharp edges
   B. No button eyes or similar parts, that can be pulled off
   C. No pieces small enough to be swallowed
   D. All materials, including paint, must be nontoxic
3. Many homemade toys can fill the same child needs as can their expensive store-bought counterparts.
4. Providing beautiful toys for children is less important than providing toys that meet needs.
5. Parents *can make* the toys children need.

## ACTIVITIES AND RESOURCES

Several toy projects are listed below. These projects are easy to do and are appropriate for several developmental stages in the preschool years. Other ideas are readily available in a number of books.

### Put and Take

Materials: Plastic ice cream or margarine containers, colored plastic tape, magazine pictures, scissors, clear contact paper, a collection of small items (e.g., comb, spoon, curler)

Directions:

1.  Cut the tape into shapes and attach to the container as decorations; or
2.  Cut out magazine pictures and glue on the outside of the container; or
3.  Cover the container with clear contact paper.

Play value: Young children and older babies delight in "putting in" and "taking out." Receptacle play starts at about 1 year of age. Labels attached to the items by the parent can also make this game a language activity. Items can be stored in the container.

### Pull Toys

Materials: 1-quart cardboard milk containers, fabric, glue, string

Directions:

1.  Clean and dry containers thoroughly.
2.  Seal opening.
3.  Glue fabric to cover containers.

One or more containers may be tied together. A long string with a spool (to hold on one end) makes this a usable pull toy.

Play value: The fabric will make this an attractive toy to look at, and the string will enable the child to pull it through the house. Beginning walkers love to drag toys with them as they go about their explorations.

### Stack and Nest

Materials: Three sizes of food cans (the cut edge should be smooth)
Paints: one yellow, one blue, one red (primary colors)
Brushes
Construction paper: yellow, blue, red squares
Small items: cars, toy people, combs

Directions:

1.  Each can should be painted one of the three primary colors.

2.   Colored plastic tape can be used to cover the cut edge.

Play value: The cans may be stacked or nested. The paper squares or items can be sorted by color and placed in the matching can. This activity offers the opportunity to begin matching the primary colors or to hear, repeat, and learn the labels for a number of small items.

### Shakers

Materials: Sand, pebbles, potato chip or juice cans, paint or construction paper

Directions:

1.   Place sand or pebbles in container.
2.   Seal lid on firmly with tape.
3.   Paint outside of container or cover with construction paper.

Play value: Older babies and children will enjoy shaking the container. If two containers (one filled with sand, one filled with pebbles) are available, the child will begin to notice the difference in sound. Parents and children can also shake to the tunes of songs they sing or to radio and television music.

### Rhythm Sticks

Materials: ¾-inch wide dowels (can be purchased by the yard at most hardware stores), sandpaper, paint, brushes

Directions:

1.   Cut dowels to desired length (8–12 inches).
2.   Sand the cut edges until smooth.
3.   Paint the sticks.

Play value: Sticks hit against each other make a satisfying clicking noise. Parents and children should each have a set. Beating the sticks to music or to the rhythm of chanted nursery rhymes can be a satisfying activity.

### REFERENCES

Accardo, P.J., & Capute, A.J. (1979). *The pediatrician and the developmentally delayed child: A clinical textbook on mental retarda-*

tion. *Monographs in developmental pediatrics* (vol. 2). Baltimore: University Park Press.

Brigance, A.H. (1978). *Brigance diagnostic inventory of early development.* North Bellerica, MA: Curriculum Associates, Inc.

Illingworth, R.S. (1967). *The development of the infant and young child: Normal and abnormal.* Baltimore: Williams & Wilkins.

Sheridan, M.D. (1968). *The developmental progress of infants and young children. London: Her Majesty's Stationery Office.*

# 6 | Parents Learning Together III

## The second generation

Joyce Coleman

## INTRODUCTION

The Parents Learning Together (PLT) Program is an innovative service that provides family support and developmental programming to adults with mental retardation/developmental disabilities and their children. This much-needed service comes at a time in society when the trends towards deinstitutionalization and normalization have provided the opportunity for individuals with mental retardation to marry, to have children, and to live independently in family units. Nonetheless, providing these opportunities does not ensure successful parenting skills or the ability to manage a household. Through the Parents Learning Together Program professionals have collected information about the strengths and needs of this special population and the successes and failures of delivering services to these families.

## HISTORY

The Parents Learning Together Program originated in 1983. It was designed by two departments of St. Louis University: the New Hope Learning Center, which runs a program for preschool children with developmental disabilities, and the Knights of Columbus Developmental Center, a facility affiliated with St. Louis University and Cardinal Glennon Hospital for the diagnosis and evaluation of handicapping conditions. The project was funded by a grant from the St. Louis Office For Mental Retardation and Developmental Disability Resources and administered by the New Hope Foundation. The initial grant provided funding for both a needs assessment to determine the approximate size of this population and a parenting program.

The pilot needs assessment identified 402 families in the St. Louis metropolitan area as being headed by an adult with mental retardation. There were a total of 1096 children represented (mean per family/parent = 2.83) of whom 601 (55%) were in the home and 495 (45%) were out of the home (either because they had been removed by the authorities or were old enough to leave the home on their own). (Whitman, Graves, Accardo, 1987)

Based on the significant number of families identified through the needs assessment, the second component of the grant, the parenting program, was developed. Both center-based and home intervention services were started with 10 families. The families all were residents of St. Louis city, a lower socioeconomic, inner city population. At that time this program was one of only three such programs in the nation.

The program continued to grow, and enrollment doubled by the third year. The need for this service was firmly established. However, due to financial considerations, the New Hope Foundation discontinued the project, and in 1986 the grant was awarded to the St. Louis Association For Retarded Citizens (ARC), which currently operates the program.

The St. Louis Association For Retarded Citizens has provided services to persons with mental retardation and developmental disabilities since 1950. The agency serves over 2000 clients per year through a broad range of services, including early childhood programs, family support, respite, adult habilitation, leisure skills training, and residential group homes. The mission of the ARC is to secure and/or provide services for individuals in the least restrictive environment, and to make sure that the services and programs offered are of the highest quality possible within the financial means of the agency. The Parents Learning Together Program is very appropriate in regard to the mission of the agency and came at a time when a strong commitment had been made to family support services.

## DEVELOPMENT OF THE PROGRAM: THE SECOND PHASE

### Case Finding

The first 3 years of the project had been devoted to identification of the population and establishing a service delivery system. The New Hope Foundation discontinued the project in June of 1986 at the end of the fiscal year; the St. Louis ARC resumed services in September of that same year. With this transition, the first lesson learned was that client families need consistency and continuity of services. In the weeks that elapsed during the transition of service providers, the families seemed to disappear. Some had moved with no forwarding addresses, while others, once located, appeared skeptical of the new personnel. Thus, much time previously planned for service was devoted to locating the client families and rebuilding relationships. Since we were new to the program, it was also important to make community contacts and establish a working relationship with previous and potential referral sources. Contacts were made with Department of Family Services (DFS), Department of Mental Health, Salvation Army, health clinics, hospitals, private physicians, visiting nurses, and other social service agencies. We found that almost all of the social service agencies contacted indicated that they worked with families who could benefit from our program and felt it to be a much-needed service.

### Staffing Pattern

The program staff initially included a director, program coordinator, and two assistants. The director was responsible for the administration of this program as well as the early childhood programs at St. Louis ARC. The program coordinator provided direct services both in the center and through home visits. The assistants were involved primarily with the center-based services. The staff began by reviewing various curricula and developing lesson plans with the intent to provide a comprehensive parent training program. What the ARC staff had not been prepared for was the need to deal with the daily family crises that took priority over the scheduled training. These crises ranged from utilities being cut off, being evicted from their homes, lack of food in the house, and emergency medical situations, to family violence. It became clear that these immediate problems had to be addressed and that this program could not be approached as a typical parent training program. By the second year we reorganized the staff to include the director to administer the program, a half-time social worker to address the many identified social service needs, a program coordinator to implement individualized family service plans (IFSPs) based on the assessed family needs, a half-time assistant to provide home intervention services, and a van driver/assistant to transport clients and assist with the center-based services. While we could justify further additional staff for this project, these key positions are essential to a program of this type.

### Service Delivery Model

The combination of center- and home-based services has proven to be the most successful mode of providing training to these families. The center-based instruction focuses on specific child care issues of nutrition, safety, behavior management, child growth and development, as well as family relations and household management. Through the center-based services the families develop friendships and receive group support. The home visits provide a time for the staff to evaluate whether the family is applying the skills that have been taught at the center and to learn more about the family and how they function as a unit. Weekly contacts have averaged at 60%–70% of the scheduled appointments. Our clients require a staff that is willing to pursue a relationship. It is often too easy for these families to become complacent with a life-style that at best offers predictability, regardless of the quality-of-life it may offer.

### Transportation

The ability of the families to get to the program or to other community resources continues to be a serious challenge. They do not own cars; in most cases they do not even have a driver's license. They frequently do not have money for public transportation, even if they know how to or feel comfortable using it. In addition, family and friends have typically been unavailable as a resource to assist them. When the program began, cab passes were purchased to get the families to and from the program, but the budget did not provide for additional transportation. During the second year, a grant was received to purchase a van for transporting the families. This has increased our ability to connect families with available community resources, although not to the extent needed. We have transported families to medical appointments, to school conferences, to apply for financial assistance, and to social events, in addition to providing transportation for trips and home from the program.

## Individualized Family Service Plans

Each individual referred to the program is given the Slosson Intelligence Test-Revised (SIT-R), as part of the intake process to determine eligibility. This is often the only testing information available. Despite the many severe learning problems they must have experienced during their early years, our clients were not referred for psychological testing or remedial education. Formal education for these families usually means being "socially" promoted through elementary school and in some cases even through high school. Very few received any special education services, and it would appear they simply slipped through the cracks of the educational system. Their ability to interact in a family and in society has been learned through life experiences. They know by rote the types of questions the social service professionals ask and the kinds of answers to respond with. Because of this, it is often difficult at first to determine an individual's functional level. We have found that most of the individuals lack basic reading skills, and they also have great difficulty with basic math and problem-solving concepts. Added to these needs are the ongoing family crisis situations, including family violence, abuse and neglect, homelessness, and medical emergencies.

Initially the curriculum materials reviewed and developed emphasized a more traditional parent training program. We soon learned that these families needed a service much broader in scope and presented at a much more basic level than we expected. We determined that each family must be assessed on an individual basis to evaluate both their strengths and needs and a family service plan must be developed that addresses those specific needs.

A process for assessment and developing IFSPs became the focus of working with these families as opposed to adopting a specific curriculum. We consulted with a family therapist to learn more about a family systems approach and to assist us in developing a tool for measuring family needs. Several weeks were spent in reviewing various materials already available for collecting information about families. These materials included surveys to measure parent-child interactions, parent stress indexes, and basic family needs inventories. The staff finally agreed to start with a very basic needs survey from which the IFSP would be written.

The survey includes six sections:

A.   Needs for Information
B.   Needs for Emotional Support
C.   Community Services
D.   Financial Needs
E.   Family Needs
F.   Other Needs/Comments

Each adult member of the family is asked to rate the items on the survey with one of three responses: 1) I do not need help with this, 2) Not sure, or 3) I do need help with this. It is important to receive input from each family member, as the perception of family needs certainly may differ from one individual to another. It has also been interesting to compare the family's rating of needs with that of the professional staff. The staff frequently view the family as having many more or different needs than what the family identifies. It is important that the staff remain objective and not impose middle-class values when striving to assist the family with improving their overall functioning.

Section A identifies informational needs related to child development and parenting. Like many people entering the role of parent, persons who have mental retardation seem to lack a clear understanding of developmental milestones; acceptable behavior at different age levels; appropriate play and social interactions; as well as more basic information regarding infant nutrition, clothing, first aid, child safety, childhood illnesses, and medical care.

Section B is aimed at identifying the family's need for emotional support. Although these individuals often live with extended family or other unrelated adults, there seems to be a lack of adequate emotional support. Perhaps this is due to the often apparent emotional neediness of the entire household, which can leave little energy for offering support to one another.

Section C presents various available community services and ratings to determine the individual's needs for these resources. The survival of the household is often dependent upon the family's ability to utilize community services. In many cases the family is unaware of the service, lacks the ability to make contact with the service provider, or is unable to cut through the often complicated bureaucracy to gain access to the service.

Financial needs are addressed under Section D. As previously mentioned, value systems are a very significant factor in the rating of needs. The staff member may view the family's financial situation as much more critical than the family does. For example, assistance for meeting expenses for housing may not be rated as a priority by the family, when in fact the family is at risk of being evicted from the dwelling. It is often a precarious balance that staff must maintain to deal with clearly at-risk situations that exist because of the parents' cognitive limitation, while trying to remain within a client self-determination/self-value framework.

Family interactions and communication are presented for rating in Section E. Often our clients grew up in dysfunctional families themselves and were exposed to poor role models in terms of developing healthy family relationships. Their current relationships with adults are frequently noncommital, based upon immediate and temporary needs, and lack the maturity to foster emotional growth.

Section F, Other Needs/Comments, provides the opportunity for the individuals to identify any needs that were omitted on the survey. The intent of the survey is for the family to provide the staff with their perception of their needs rather than the staff determining the needs. Depending upon the rapport the staff member has developed with the family, a great deal of information can be gathered through this survey.

Once the survey is completed, the staff selects two or three needs that the family agrees are priorities to begin working on. From this an IFSP is developed that includes objectives and time frames for meeting the identified needs. The greatest difficulty the staff have had in meeting the objectives is the constant problematic situations these families experience, which force reprioritizing needs.

## CHARACTERISTICS OF THE POPULATION

There are some characteristics that seem imperative to note for anyone who might consider developing a program for parents who have mental retardation. However, it is also important to clarify that this particular program serves a designated population area, which is inner city and low income.

Twenty-eight families are currently enrolled in the PLT Program. The parents range in age from 18–40. These 28 families represent 74 (mean per family = 2.8) children, newborn to 23 years of age. Of the 74 children, 61 live at home and 13 live outside of the home. Twenty-five of the families are headed by single mothers and three are two-parent families. In some cases the father remains in contact with the family but primarily for financial reasons. Public assistance checks are received on the first of the month, and the father may come home for a week or two and then leave again with the money.

Adults entering the program are screened with the SIT-R as well as a formal parent interview. The SIT-R results have ranged from 34–76 (mean score = 60). The preschool children have been administered the Bayley Scales of Infant Development and/or the Peabody Motor Scales. Upon entry to the program it appeared from observation that every child would exhibit delays in at least one area of development. In many cases behavior and ability to attend were interfering with the child's overall developmental functioning. The testing was completed after the families had been enrolled in the program for 6 months or longer. We found only six out of 20 children 5 years old and under to have significant developmental delay. The staff credited the positive test scores, at least in part, to the structure provided by the program, to which the entire family responded well. The six children with significant delays have been enrolled in the St. Louis ARC Early Childhood Programs. This program provides services to children birth to five years of age who are demonstrating a 6-month or presumed 6-month delay in one or more areas of development, including speech/-language, fine motor, gross motor, cognition, social emotional, or self-care. We continue to track the patterns of development for all of the children in the PLT Program on a quarterly basis.

Parenting issues seem to revolve around the ability to learn new skills and then generalizing those skills into the everyday caretaking of their children. Simply due to their intellectual limitations, these parents find certain basic concepts difficult. An example is selecting the amount and type of food to meet the nutritional needs of their children. Once they learn the concept, they may overgeneralize or undergeneralize the application of it. Another example might be learning how to select appropriate play clothes for the child and then generalizing that to the various seasons and temperatures of the physical environment. And, of course, some concepts are much more subjective and abstract, like family relationships and management of behaviors.

Parents with mental retardation may have had more practice than the average family in living with extreme stress factors, but that does not mean they have become desensitized to this life-style or developed more capacity to cope. They also find themselves presented with the same issues most families in society are challenged by. One of the married couples shared their concern over role responsibilities. The husband, on the one hand, had a very traditional view of how his spouse should function as a wife and mother. She, on the other hand, had decided to pursue her high school diploma and wanted a more liberated role. Since both are very concrete thinkers, the ability to resolve conflicting wants/needs is not well developed. Thus managing difficulties such as this is hard for them to understand, and even simple differences escalate into major family problems.

These parents' general attitude toward their children is one of acceptance and love. As in all families, they struggle with parenting and use the only model they know, their own childhood. Because of their intellectual limitations, they need the support and guidance of a program such as PLT if they are to be successful parents.

More time and money needs to be devoted to research and services for parents with mental retardation. We must better understand how intellectual limitations have an impact upon their parenting abilities and how professionals can best intervene to assist these individuals to adequately function as parents. Access to medical care, including genetic counseling and birth control, needs to be made available for these families. And finally, vocational training and employment opportunities must be part of a comprehensive training program.

## SUMMARY

The staff must continually reevaluate and measure the effectiveness of the services being provided to these families. However, some families who entered this program at risk of losing their children due to abusive and neglectful circumstances are now successfully maintaining their family units. Developmental assessments document that the majority of the preschool children are functioning at age level; we attribute this to the increased stimulation the parents are providing as a result of skills gained through the program. We know that these persons can and want to learn parenting and have accomplished the objectives negotiated in their IFSPs. Intervention is making a difference in the lives of these families and is an important investment in the future for a society that has embraced the philosophy of least restrictive environment, community integration, and full citizenship for individuals with mental retardation.

## REFERENCES

Whitman, B., Graves, B., & Accardo, P. (1987). Mentally retarded parents in the community: Identification method and needs assessment survey. *American Journal of Mental Deficiency, 91* (6), 636–638.

# IV

## Children of Parents with Mental Retardation

# 7 | Children of Parents with Mental Retardation

## Problems and diagnoses

Pasquale J. Accardo
Barbara Y. Whitman

Cognitive limitation in a parent has long been recognized as a risk factor for abuse and neglect in children (Crain & Millor, 1978; Schilling, Schinke, Blythe, & Barth, 1982; Seagull & Scheurer, 1986; Sheridan, 1956). Our research has shown that children of parents with mental retardation have a high rate of removal from the family of origin and that abuse seems more likely to occur with decreasing parental IQ and with increasing child IQ. This suggests the importance of cognitive dissonance or a severe intellectual mismatch between parent and child. Larger family size and the absence of a supportive family network also appeared to represent significant contributions to the evolution of dysfunctional parent-child interactions.

## THE POPULATION SAMPLED

Over a 6-year period 1,275 children were referred to the Knights of Columbus Developmental Center at Cardinal Glennon Children's Hospital, St. Louis, Missouri, for the assessment of problems in development and behavior. During that time 107 of the children were noted to have at least one parent with mental retardation. Chapter 7 reviews the child and parent variables in these family units. Because of the descriptive nature of the data, results will be offered in terms of percentages without any more elaborate analysis of statistical significance (Accardo & Whitman, 1989).

The 107 children were from 79 families, each of which had between one and nine children (mean 2.9, standard deviation 1.9, with a total of 226 children, Figure 7.1). A little under one third of these 107 children (31%) were themselves diagnosed as having mental retardation. At the time of their evaluation, family size ranged from 0 to 6 children (mean 1.6, standard deviation 1.5, Figure 7.2). For a variety of reasons (i.e., given up for adoption; removed by Division of Family/Protective Services for child abuse, child neglect, sexual abuse, unsafe living conditions), 103 children were no longer in the home. With only 123 of the 226 biological children still residing in the home, there was a removal rate of 45.6%. This figure may represent a slightly low estimate for several reasons. First, the mothers

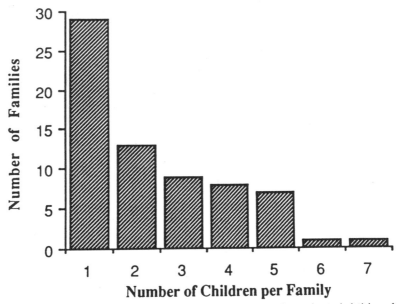

Figure 7.1.   Number of children per family. (Reported number of children for each of 79 families with a parent who has mental retardation. For the reasons described in the text the total of 226 children needs to be regarded as an approximation.)

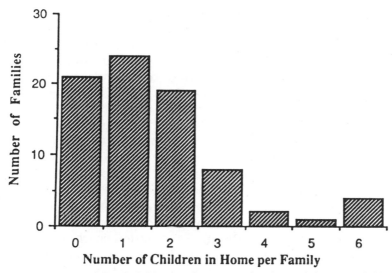

Figure 7.2.    Number of children in home per family. (Of the 226 children reported in Figure 7.1, 103 had been previously removed from the family of origin. The distribution of the remaining 123 among the 79 families is depicted here. Note that there are now 21 families with no children in the home.)

were not always certain of the exact number of children that they had given birth to, the number that had been removed, or the number that had died. Second, the initial diagnostic classification of mental retardation in the parent was being made for the first time with a number of these clients. If this risk factor had been identified earlier it might have contributed to a higher removal rate.

The most difficult parameter to assess was the level of mental retardation in the parent(s). In some cases the diagnosis was made by reviewing the parental school records; in other cases the parent described the type of special education placement he or she had experienced. In selected cases IQ test data were available from school records or court-ordered psychiatric evaluations; in some cases full IQ testing or Slosson Intelligence Test-Revised (SIT-R) screenings were administered in the clinic. Appropriate consent for both release of information and testing remained problematical. Whenever possible the record information and test data were correlated with the parental adult functional state and level of adaptive performance. Thus, some parents who had previously been identified as having mental retardation were noted on clinical interview and assessment to have a learning, social interaction, employment history, or speech pattern more compatible with a language disability or specific learning disability. These parents and those with other undiagnosed problems, such as deafness and major psychiatric disorders, were not included in the present group. In a number of cases parents were not available for interview when the children had previously been removed from the home (with no intention of working to return them to the biological parents) or the parents were, for various other reasons, not cooperating in the assessment process (in one case the child had been placed out of the home at birth, and detailed maternal records were available from the adoption agency.) Parents with mental retardation who themselves had additional diagnoses were not excluded. With one exception, all the index parents with mental retardation were mothers; there were an additional 15 fathers with mental retardation. The data presented focus on the maternal index cases, since the fathers were rarely cooperative and paternal data remained sketchy. In most cases the mothers were single or separated from the fathers.

There was a slight tendency for older children to exhibit an increased incidence of developmental diagnoses. For the 35 children age 6 years and over, the mean number of developmental diagnoses was 2.2 (standard deviation 0.9); for the 72 children age 5 years and younger, the mean number of developmental diagnoses was 1.9 (standard deviation 1.2). It would not be appropriate to interpret this increase in the incidence of developmental diagnoses with increasing child age as necessarily secondary to the child's home environment since some major diagnostic categories (e.g., specific learning disability) cannot be accurately entertained until later in childhood. However, the lower total number of older children seen may reflect a number of contributing explanations: a greater facility with the parenting role as the children get older, an increased reproductive rate for mentally retarded adults in the community, and an increasing rate of removal of children from parents with mental retardation as their incapacity to meet the needs of older children becomes more obvious.

## RISK FACTORS FOR CHILD ABUSE AND NEGLECT

To be considered separately from the issue of removal of the child from the home was the occurrence of child abuse, child neglect, and child sexual abuse. Some children who had been victims of such abuse/neglect had nevertheless been returned to their biological parents after Division of Family/Protective Services criteria for support services and monitoring had been met. In all, 71 of the 107 children (66.4%) had suffered some form of abuse/neglect.

Child and family variables were investigated to attempt to clarify risk factors, particularly those relevant to parental mental retardation with a special focus on the contribution to developmental disorders in the children. Table 7.1 suggests that when the children of parents with mental retardation are themselves mentally retarded or have lower IQ scores, they are less likely to be abused. Similarly, the presence of a diagnosis of language disorder or a lower verbal IQ also lowered the likelihood of abuse. However, with regard to the latter risk factor, receptive language scores (as measured by the Peabody Picture Vocabulary Test-Revised, [PPVT-R] [Dunn & Dunn, 1981]) were not strikingly different between abused children and nonabused children, and most of the discrepancy with regard to language disorders was secondary to a higher incidence of early infantile autism and expressive language disorders in the nonabused group. Autism is interpreted as more of an organic brain dysfunction syndrome (Farber & Capute, 1984), while many of the cases of purely mild expressive language disorder (often complicated by disarticulation) are probably secondary to the linguistically deprivational environment in which these children are raised. In general, the children who were cognitively brighter and could talk better seemed more likely to be abused. It is also of interest to note that all of the three cases of psychogenic water drinking occurred in the abused group (Accardo, Caul, & Whitman, 1989). Finally, regardless of the presence or absence of abuse or neglect, there was a tendency for the verbal IQ and the PPVT-R scores to be lower than the performance IQ and full-scale IQ scores. Whether this reflects more a genetic or environmental influence remains to be explored.

Investigating the impact of parental intelligence levels presented some difficulties because IQ scores and accurate functional level descriptors were not always available. In addition, much of the parental information was obtained from a diversity of sources. The overall trend was, nevertheless, for parents of more limited intelligence or with a history of more restrictive educational placement experiences to be somewhat overly represented in the abuse group. Thus for the 36 children with no record of child abuse/neglect, 15 of their parents had a mean IQ

Table 7.1. The presence/absence of child abuse in families with parents who have mental retardation

| Factor | N = 107 No. | Percent | No abuse n = 36 No. | Percent | Abuse n = 71 No. | Percent |
|---|---|---|---|---|---|---|
| Mean age (child) | 5.3 | | 5.8 | | 5.0 | |
| Male | 50 | 47 | 16 | 44 | 34 | 48 |
| White | 42 | 39 | 9 | 25 | 33 | 47 |
| Learning disability | 23 | 22 | 9 | 25 | 14 | 20 |
| Attention deficit disorder (mis-diagnosed) | | 13 (17) | | 25 (17) | | 7 (17) |
| Mental retarda-tion | | 31 | | 37 | | 28 |
| Motor diagnosis | | 9 | | 8 | | 10 |
| Autism | | 3 | | 8 | | 0 |
| Disarticulation | | 36 | | 42 | | 34 |
| Language disor-der (expressive) | | 10 | | 14 | | 9 |
| Language disor-der (expressive and receptive) | | 22 | | 22 | | 23 |
| Emotional diag-nosis | | 17 | | 11 | | 20 |
| Adjustment disor-der | | 8 | | 6 | | 10 |
| Psychogenic wa-ter drinking | 3 | 2 | | 0 | 3 | 4 |
| Family diagnosis depression | | 9 | | 8 | | 10 |
| Family diagnosis severe psycho-pathology | | 21 | | 6 | | 28 |
| IQ (child) mean | (n = 105) | 68.8 | (n = 34) | 65.4 | (n = 71) | 70.4 |
| SD | | 18.7 | | 20.2 | | 17.9 |
| P-V mean | (n = 29) | 9.8 | (n = 12) | 15.3 | (n = 17) | 6.0 |
| SD | | 18.0 | | 17.6 | | 17.9 |
| PPVT-R mean | (n = 61) | 64.2 | (n = 18) | 65.0 | (n = 43) | 63.9 |
| SD | | 17.2 | | 19.3 | | 16.5 |

All the children appear to exhibit some degree of language or verbal limitation. Less than one third (31%) of the children have mental retardation although diagnosis by IQ score alone would have markedly increased that percentage. Brighter and more verbal children appear to be at greater risk for some form of abuse or neglect. All three instances of psychogenic water drinking occurred in the abused group.

of 55.1 (standard deviation 10.6, range 37–69), and the other
21 index parents had the following educational history: EMR 1
(educable mentally retarded), TMR 5 (trainable mentally retarded), SPMR (severe and profound mentally retarded) 1, "special education" 13, and unspecified 1. For the 71 children with
a history of abuse/neglect 21 of their parents had a mean IQ of
52.8 (standard deviation 7.8, range 33–65), and the remaining
50 index parents had the following educational history: EMR 2,
TMR 13, SPMR 7, "special education" 15, and unspecified 13.
When correlating a higher incidence of child abuse/neglect
with lower parental IQ, the following confounding effect must
be allowed for: the ability to successfully conceal child abuse
probably varies directly with parental intelligence level.

When parents have mental retardation and experience a
multiplicity of other life stresses that are frequently associated
with mental retardation, one can reasonably anticipate that
family size (i.e., number of children) will probably have a major
impact on the limited ability of these parents to cope with the
added stress of childrearing. When family size was cross-tabu-
lated against the percentages of children placed in foster care,
sexually abused, failing to thrive (FTT), or abused and neglected (Table 7.2), there were clear trends for an increase in
the number of children in the family to parallel an increase in
incidence of these child problems as well as for the percentage
of children with none of these abuse/neglect problems to de-
crease with increasing family size.

Clinical impression suggested that the nature of the personal support network available to parents with mental retardation would be a major determining factor in the incidence of
identifiable abuse/neglect in the children. Table 7.3 supports
the accuracy of this observation for 91 of the 107 children; the
other 16 children were in families receiving intensive agency
services. Comparing no support network or a second parent

Table 7.2.  Family size and child abuse/neglect

| Family size (children) | 1–2 | | 3–4 | | >4 | |
|---|---|---|---|---|---|---|
| N | 48 | Percent | 28 | Percent | 31 | Percent |
| Foster homes | 20 | 42 | 10 | 36 | 24 | 77 |
| Sexual abuse | 1 | 2 | 6 | 21 | 8 | 26 |
| FTT | 14 | 29 | 10 | 36 | 13 | 42 |
| Abuse/neglect | 15 | 31 | 16 | 57 | 21 | 68 |
| No problems | 22 | 46 | 9 | 32 | 5 | 16 |

Table 7.3. Personal support network and child abuse/neglect

| Support | None | Second MR parent | Non-MR parent | Other relatives |
|---|---|---|---|---|
| N | 36 | 20 | 9 | 26 |
| Foster home | 24 (67%) | 13 (65%) | 2 (22%) | 11 (42%) |
| Sexual abuse | 9 (25%) | 6 (32%) | 0 (0%) | 0 (0%) |
| FTT | 13 (36%) | 8 (40%) | 4 (44%) | 8 (31%) |
| Abuse/neglect | 20 (56%) | 14 (70%) | 3 (33%) | 12 (46%) |
| No problems | 10 (28%) | 2 (10%) | 3 (33%) | 13 (50%) |

with mental retardation, on the one hand, with a second parent or other relative who does not have mental retardation, on the other hand, most of the group differences were in the expected direction and on the order of magnitude of factors of 2–3.

Consider the following instance of child abuse and neglect involving parents with mental retardation. A 4½-year-old girl presented to the General Pediatric Service for routine health maintenance. She was noted to be obese (weight of 11 standard deviations above the mean for age) and hypertensive. There was further concern that she had significant mental retardation because of her uncontrollable tantrumming behavior in the outpatient clinic setting. Developmental Pediatrics was consulted to rule out Prader-Willi syndrome or Sotos syndrome. The child did not fit minimal diagnostic criteria for any syndromic diagnosis and was not felt to have mental retardation. Her behavior was a reflection of the total inability of her two mentally retarded parents to effectively set any limits on her, and her obesity mirrored the parental reliance on food reinforcers to maintain a semblance of peace in the home. After 6 months of multiple agency interventions to help these parents set limits and provide dietary regulation, the girl's weight increased to 13 standard deviations above the mean for age, and she was described as having episodes that fit the clinical picture of sleep apnea. In the same interval a sibling was born, and it was discovered that the first child was being sexually abused by an unidentified member of the family's large and chaotic household. Since the court equated malnutrition with the classic sign of parental neglect, the health crisis relating to her obesity had been insufficient to obtain this child's removal to an appropriate environment. The sexual abuse incident, which was probably precipitated by the birth of the sibling, brought about her placement in a structured environment where both her behavior and eating habits were more amenable to modification. The misinterpretation of the obesity as a sign of well-intentioned, but misguided, caring for this child delayed appropriate placement long after the critical seriousness of the medical problem was noted. This child's situation illustrates the complex interactions among the factors contributing to child abuse when a parent has mental retardation.

## REFERENCES

Accardo, P.J., Caul, J., & Whitman, B.Y. Excessive water drinking in children. *Clinical Pediatrics.* (in press).

Accardo, P.J., & Whitman, B.Y. (1989). Factors influencing child abuse/neglect in children of mentally retarded parents. *Pediatric Research, 25,* 95A (abstract 256).

Crain, L.S., & Millor, G.K. (1978). Forgotten children: Maltreated children of mentally retarded parents. *Pediatrics, 61,* 130–132.

Dunn, L., & Dunn, L. (1981). *Peabody Picture Vocabulary Test—revised: Manual for Forms L and M.* Circle Pines, MN: American Guidance Service.

Farber, J.M., & Capute, A.J. (1984). Understanding autism. *Clinical Pediatrics, 23,* 199–202.

Seagull, E.A.W., & Scheurer, S.L. (1986). Neglected and abused children of mentally retarded parents. *Child Abuse & Neglect, 10,* 493–500.

Schilling, R.F., Schinke, S.P., Blythe, B.J., & Barth, R.P. (1982). Child maltreatment and mentally retarded parents: Is there a relationship? *Mental Retardation, 20,* 201–209.

Sheridan, M.D. (1956). The intelligence of 100 neglectful mothers. *British Journal of Medicine, 1,* 91–92.

# 8 | Children of Parents with Mental Retardation

## The pediatrician's role

Ursula T. Rolfe

## INTRODUCTION

"The pediatrician's commitment is to secure for all children the opportunity to achieve their full native potential" (Behrman & Vaughn, 1987, p. 1).

This challenging commitment can feel overwhelming, especially since the present climate of "the business of medicine" with its emphasis on "efficiency" and "assembly line scheduling" makes it difficult for pediatricians to devote the time and energy necessary to help children with complicated problems. Children with chronic diseases, growth failure, developmental delays, and those with unexplained signs and symptoms often require in-depth histories and examinations as well as time for reading, reflection, and consultation with colleagues. Such special children need, and deserve, a larger investment of the pediatrician's time and energy than the more usual patient with acute febrile illness or minor injury. A child who is cared for by a parent with mental retardation is also one of these special children. Chapter 8 contains suggestions for the practicing pediatrician on how to deal with children of parents with mental retardation. It includes clues to identify parents with mental retardation and guidelines for evaluating and managing the child and family, as well as collaborating with nurses, social workers, and other professionals, both in the physician's office and in the community.

## PARENTS WITH MENTAL RETARDATION

A parent with mental retardation who brings a child to the pediatrician will usually function in the range of mild mental retardation to borderline functioning. Mild mental retardation is usually not genetically determined, and the majority of offspring conceived by parents with mild mental retardation will have the potential for normal intellectual and social development. Yet many such children never reach that potential, either because of adverse intrauterine or perinatal events or because of inadequate nurturing, protection, and stimulation during infancy and childhood (Farran & McKinney, 1986; Garber, 1988). At times both pre- and postnatal factors may hinder normal development.

## RISK FACTORS

Many women with mental retardation live in poor economic circumstances, and have little knowledge or understanding of how to safeguard their own health, or how to utilize the health care available for their children. Mothers with mental retardation may not receive optimal obstetric care, either through ignorance or unavailability. Thus, their offspring tend to be at higher than usual risk for intrauterine insults such as infection, exposure to noxious substances (e.g., lead, alcohol) malnutrition, lack of prenatal care, and other intrauterine and perinatal complications.

Postnatal risk factors pertain primarily to the parents' cognitive, social, and emotional development, and to the available economic and social support. Parents with mental retardation may lack the knowledge and skills necessary to provide for their child's physical and emotional needs. They may not be able to understand or follow instructions regarding everyday activities or to attend to special needs such as the administration of medications. This is especially true if instructions are in writing and the parent is at most semiliterate. Economic resources to provide for food, clothing, and shelter are frequently inadequate, and parents may not be able to use available money prudently.

These parents may find it difficult to provide their children with the chance to explore their environment, while also setting appropriate limits for their safety and socialization. Such parents may also be unable to stimulate their children's cognitive and verbal skills, answer their numerous questions, and encourage learning by providing stimulation and approval (Boodoosingh & Brown, 1986).

An additional difficulty is that parents with mental retardation may have unrealistic expectations of their children's abilities and may be emotionally immature and have low tolerance for frustration. These factors can result in under- or overprotection and lead to accidental injuries and poisoning as well as physical, emotional, or sexual abuse, and exploitation or assault by others (Whitman, Graves, & Accardo, 1987). In addition, many people with mental retardation have themselves suffered mental, physical, or sexual abuse and may thus perpetuate cycles of abuse.

Nevertheless, many such parents who are given proper guidance and support are able to be adequate and loving parents to one or two children. Too frequently, however, these parents are overwhelmed with multiple pregnancies in rapid succession. The resultant increasing demands are accompanied by emotional, social, and physical depletion. Limited understanding of family planning and difficulty in compliance with family planning methods increase the risk of inadequate parenting due to depletion of parental resources. A concise and helpful discussion of the issues of sexuality and contraception for persons with mental retardation is found in Hall (1975).

## THE PEDIATRICIAN'S ROLE

The care of children who live with parents who have mental retardation presents a special challenge to the pediatrician and his or her staff. Necessary tasks are multiple. One must first identify the developmentally disabled parents. The professional must then evaluate the child to determine possible genetic, intrauterine, or perinatal conditions that identify the child to be at increased risk for mental retardation. Further, the doctor must assess the caregiver's parenting skills and clarify the nature of parental support systems. He or she must become familiar with community resources in order to act as an advocate for the child and family, making appropriate referrals for assistance with economic needs and parental health needs including sex education and birth control, general life skills, and instruction in parenting. When the child's needs for physical and mental development cannot be met in the biological parents' home, the pediatrician must be an active participant in the choice of an alternative living environment.

The ability of parents with mental retardation to attend to the basic needs of their infants and toddlers depends not only on their intellectual capacities but also on their personalities and childhood experiences. While parents with mild mental retardation and most of those in the borderline range are able to respond to their infants' needs for feeding, cleaning, warmth, and affection with little guidance and supervision, the needs of the toddler and preschool child are more complicated. Preschool children need not only opportunities and encouragement to explore their environment, but also socialization experiences and appropriate limits to be set for protection. They also need stimulation to increase their cognitive and verbal skills, and answers to their numerous questions. Parents with mental retardation will need considerable help in fulfilling these needs of the preschool child. Parenting classes and in-home supervision as well as nursery school and day-care programs should be used to supplement the parents' efforts.

## INTERACTION WITH PARENTS

Evaluation of parenting skills is an important part of any pediatric office visit. This starts when parent and child arrive in the office. Nurse and physician should share their observations of parent-child interaction; the parent's facility in handling, feeding, undressing, and dressing the infant or toddler; and the parent's ability to comfort the hurt or frightened child. Other important observations include the parent's response to an infant's smile, vocalizations, and other interactional cues, as well as protective reactions such as guarding the infant when on an examining table. Parental expectations of the infant's or child's abilities should be assessed, and corrected, if necessary.

Unrealistic attitudes of parents with mental retardation may include the expectations that small infants should be fed only three times per day and sleep throughout the night. They may unreasonably expect toilet training to be accomplished by age 12 months, and a 2-year-old to be as responsible and obedient as a school-age child. Correction of such misperceptions is essential in order to avoid misguided attempts at teaching or discipline. The parent's tolerance for normal developmental behavior such as infant crying or oppositional behavior by a 2-year-old must also be assessed. Simple questions asked in a gentle, empathic manner are helpful in eliciting this information, for example, "How old do you think Jody will be when she starts using the potty or toilet?" "What do you do when Jimmy keeps crying at night?" "What do you do when you feel angry at Mary?"

The initial visit will usually reveal the mother's mental retardation because she will be unable to provide intelligent answers to questions regarding her pregnancy, labor, or delivery, and may be vague or clearly wrong about her infant's newborn course, the type and amount of feeding, or the child's development. Inability to answer questions about her past history, family history, former place of residence, and schooling will also help to reveal her cognitive limitations. Difficulty in recalling all sorts of numbers is very prominent; examples include dates of births, birth weights, addresses, and telephone numbers. In some cases parents, in an effort to hide their limitations and protect themselves from ridicule, may appear hostile or withdrawn and disinterested. The pediatrician should supplement the parent's history with records from the parent's health care providers as well as from family members wherever possible. The parent's school record may provide information regarding cognitive ability and behavioral traits, as well as otherwise unavailable medical information.

Important aspects of the medical family history concern any factors that may be related to the cause of the parent's mental retardation. This includes the presence of a known genetic disease, mental retardation in other members of the family, epilepsy, or sensory deficits that might help to estimate risk of recurrence in the child as well as the need for genetic, metabolic, or other studies. Equally important would be a history indicating that the parent's cognitive limitations are caused by nonheritable events such as central nervous system infection, major head trauma, or prolonged anoxia.

Prenatal history must include inquiry regarding the mother's general health, the number of prenatal visits (if any), the presence of seizure disorder or other chronic disease, the mother's use of medications (especially anticonvulsants), as well as the use of alcohol, street drugs, and presence of sexually transmitted diseases. Inquiry about the number of previous pregnancies, live births, general health, growth and development of previous children, and whether these offspring are living with the parent, may give valuable insight into the parent's ability to function.

## INTERACTION WITH THE CHILD

Physical examination may reveal the presence of dysmorphic features, including microcephaly, signs of fetal exposure to alcohol or anticonvulsants, or skin findings indicative of neurocutaneous syndromes. An excellent description of physical findings suggestive of mental retardation associated with hereditary or intrauterine factors can be found in Accardo and Caf)ute (1979).

The infant or child who is unkempt, dirty, and has neglected skin lesions raises suspicion of parental neglect due to parental incompetence. It is therefore important to inquire about socioeconomic circumstances; for example, lack of hot water in an unheated house could be a major reason for such findings. The presence of a large bald spot on the back of the head (occiput) of an infant frequently indicates lack of attention. Bruises, scars (especially linear ones), burns, and fractures must always be evaluated as to etiology. They may be the result of inappropriate physical punishment (e.g., excessive spanking and beatings, or, in some cases biting a small child in order to teach him or her not to bite), underprotection resulting in repeated injuries, or uncontrolled parental anger resulting in physical abuse. Examination of external genitalia for signs of abnormality or inflammation should be accompanied by simple instructions for cleansing and clear information as to who should be allowed to touch the child's genitalia.

Careful assessment of growth and development may reveal much about the adequacy of the child's environment. The infant or child who is well developed, well nourished, and displays normal affect and attainment of developmental milestones, should elicit the physician's praise for the good job the parents are doing. The parents should be encouraged to ask questions about the infant or child, and detailed anticipatory guidance must also be given.

The infant or child who is failing to thrive needs careful evaluation to determine organic as well as environmental causes. Frequently, organic abnormalities such as GE (gastroesophageal) reflux, CNS (central nervous system) immaturity, or other physical abnormalities may cause the infant to be irritable or apathetic, which, in turn, may elicit parental feelings of anxiety, frustration, or disinterest. Developmental delays must be carefully assessed. A lack of stimulation in infancy will affect development of vocalization and verbalization more markedly than motor skills. Development of language skills (including preverbal vocalizations) is thought to be the best predictor of cognitive development. Formal testing of children with parents who have mental retardation has shown noticeable language delays as early as 2 years of age. Not surprisingly, such delays appeared to be associated with decreased verbal interactions between parent and child (Feldman, 1986). Although global psychomotor retardation may be seen in children who have experienced severe emotional deprivation, it is more frequently the result of congenital factors or brain insults.

Identification of developmental delays should prompt evaluation for possible sensory limitations and neurologic abnormalities. Referral for more specialized evaluation by a developmental pediatrician, ophthalmologist, audiologist, or neurologist may be indicated.

Most of these infants and toddlers will need additional stimulation. Infant-parent programs for persons who have mental retardation are becoming increasingly available and have been shown to result in better parenting skills which have been maintained over a period of many months (Feldman, 1986). Additional resources such as day-care centers, nursery schools, and other preschool programs should be utilized to increase stimulation and socialization of these children, preferably before developmental delays occur. Transportation must be made available when needed and attendance monitored.

## MANAGEMENT OF THE PARENT-CAREGIVER

When caring for the child of a parent with mental retardation, the pediatrician or his or her staff must take the time to give

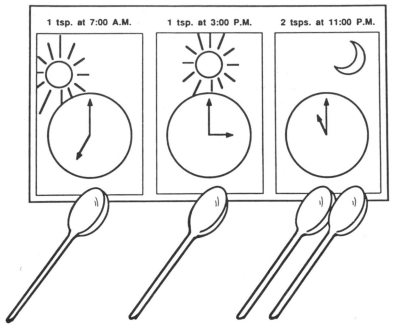

| 1 tsp. at 7:00 A.M. | 1 tsp. at 3:00 P.M. | 2 tsps. at 11:00 P.M. |

Figure 8.1.   Sample of drawing to illustrate use of pictures in giving directions to parents who are illiterate. This drawing uses the face of a clock and the sun and moon to illustrate the time at which medication is to be given, and the spoons to show the amount.

needed instructions to the parents in detail, by demonstration if possible, and to make certain they are understood. Pictorial representations are frequently helpful. For example, when medication is to be given at certain times, a picture of a clock set at the appointed time can be drawn (see Figure 8.1). Liberal use of encouragement and praise is especially important when dealing with parents who have mental retardation.

## SUPPORT SYSTEMS

Identification of parental support systems is crucial to the provision of comprehensive care. Availability of a close relative or friend who does not have mental disability may be most helpful, especially if he or she is willing and able to accept the responsibility of guiding and supervising the parent. The pediatrician and his or her staff must become familiar with available community resources. Initially, appropriate referrals may be made to state family and children's services, community agencies for citizens with mental retardation, and public or private home health nursing agencies. Other community resources that may be utilized include parent aides who provide emotional support to parents and teach them parenting skills in the home, homemakers, parenting courses, day-care centers and nursery schools. Group homes may be especially valuable for some families. These group homes accommodate several families who live in a communal, supervised setting. Parents receive help in developing parenting skills and other life skills, while needed stimulation and security are provided for the children.

Since many families will need support from several sources, a primary caseworker is essential to ensure that needed services are provided, to avoid duplication and confusion, and to act as a liaison between family and service providers. The parent should be able to contact the caseworker when the need arises and should have explicit and understandable directions on how to manage forseeable emergencies such as illness or injury of a child or parent, or what steps to take when feeling overwhelmed and unable to cope. Once the caseworker has been identified, the pediatrician should schedule a meeting with that person. This may be coordinated with an office visit for the child and his or her parents. This meeting can serve not only to discuss the family's present needs, but also to define just what responsibilities the support person will take on, and how this person, the family, and the pediatrician will communicate. Many community or life skills caseworkers who attempt to promote independence of their clients will encourage parents to visit the physician on their own. This may deprive both the pediatrician and the caseworker of needed information unless other routes of communication are agreed upon.

The pediatrician should arrange regular follow-up visits to monitor the child's growth and development, as well as suggest changes in the parent-child interaction as the child's physical and cognitive abilities develop. The pediatrician should continue to be an advocate for the child and family. When the child's needs are not being met, the doctor must take the time to communicate with appropriate individuals or agencies and clearly and forcefully express a professional opinion regarding the child's needs and the probable long-term consequences of not meeting them.

## ADVOCACY

When adequate educational, economic, or social resources are unavailable, the physician should not hesitate to challenge the community and its leaders. If society safeguards the right of persons with mental retardation to raise their own children, then society is also responsible for guaranteeing that these children have the emotional, environmental, economic, and educational conditions to enable them to reach their intellectual potential, and society will benefit.

Pediatricians can be important advocates for children (and families) in their community. Their opinions will usually be listened to, especially when given in a spirit of cooperation. They should acknowledge the agencies' efforts and problems, while challenging any erroneous notion that nothing more can be done. When dealing with government agencies, the principles of dealing with families should apply: the physician should identify strengths and weaknesses and recognize accomplishments as well as identifying shortcomings. When families neglect or abuse their children, pediatricians frequently seek assistance from the courts; the same strategy should apply to government agencies that neglect or abuse children for whose well-being they are responsible (Goldstein, Freud, & Solnit, 1979).

Responsible use of public media is often a potent tool in efforts to improve services for children. The pediatrician should not hesitate to use the media for this purpose but must be mindful of the patient's right to privacy. Since the media may try to attract attention by exaggerating reported incidents or quoting statements out of context, the pediatrician is advised to insist on reviewing articles and editing interviews before they are released to the public.

## FAMILY PLANNING

Parents who have mental retardation need ongoing help in deciding on the number of offspring they are able to care for and the optimal spacing of their children, as well as help in deciding on methods by which to avoid unplanned pregnancies. Many persons with mental retardation have received inadequate or no sex education and may have little or no understanding of birth control. The pediatrician, in his or her role as educator and advocate for the child and family, has the opportunity, as well as obligation, to facilitate needed family planning services.

The pediatrician can initiate a brief discussion about family planning at the first visit. If this initial visit takes place in the prenatal or postpartum period, the pediatrician should emphasize the importance of avoiding pregnancy in order to foster the well-being of the infant and mother. Referral to an appropriate family planning resource for necessary sex education and assessment for the best method of birth control should not be delayed. A telephone call by the physician or nurse to the family planning educators to explain the needs of the mother who has mental retardation will increase the chance for successful family planning. The family's identified community caseworker should be made aware of such a referral to ensure its successful follow-through (Craft & Craft, 1983; Fisher, Krajicek, & Borthik, 1980). If necessary, a public health nurse should be employed to help maintain appropriate compliance.

Although the pediatrician will, under ordinary circumstances, not be the parent's physician, he or she should urge the use of long-acting birth control methods. The use of oral contraceptives or barrier methods requires understanding, motivation, and planning, which are difficult for the majority of women with mental retardation. Studies such as those by Chamberlain, Rauh, Passer, McGrath and Burket (1984) and Passer, Rauh, Chamberlain, McGrath and Burket (1984) evaluated the effectiveness of different methods of birth control in women with mental retardation and found oral or barrier contraceptives to be the least satisfactory. These researchers interviewed parents of 69 adolescent girls with mental retardation to determine the parents' satisfaction with different methods of birth control. On a scale of 1–5, oral contraceptives received the lowest rating (2.7) compared with IUDs (5.0) and medroxyprogesterone acetate (Depo Provera or DMPA) (4.0). Reasons cited for the dissatisfaction included pregnancy, physical or behavioral changes ascribed to oral contraceptives, breakthrough bleeding, and the effort needed to supervise daily administration of the tablets. Parents of girls with moderate to severe mental retardation stressed the benefits of menstrual suppression with the use of DMPA, because many of these young women had difficulty in learning menstrual hygiene. Presently the use of Depo Provera or an IUD are the only long-acting methods available (Craft & Craft, 1983). Other options may become available in the future. These methods and their advantages and disadvantages are summarized in Table 8.1.

For persons with mental retardation who clearly do not wish to have more children, tubal ligation or vasectomy should be recommended. The ethical and moral questions relating to sterilization for persons with moderate or severe mental retardation, especially when the mental retardation is known to be genetically transmitted, are difficult to solve. Chamberlain et al. (1984) found that 32 (46%) of 69 parents had considered sterilization, either by tubal ligation or hysterectomy. The majority of the 69 parents favored a statute allowing sterilization for women with mental retardation under some circumstances and with certain safeguards. They felt that most women with

Table 8.1.   Contraceptives

| Method | Advantages | Disadvantages |
|---|---|---|
| Oral<br>  Estrogen-progester-<br>    one combination,<br>    progesterone only | Effective when used<br>  regularly<br>Periods regular, de-<br>  crease in cramps<br>  and blood loss | Need motivation<br>Medical contraindica-<br>  tions |
| Barrier methods<br>  Diaphragm, con-<br>    dom, cervical cap | Few complications<br>Some protection from<br>  STDs<br>Quite effective when<br>  used correctly | Need to plan ahead;<br>  not good for imma-<br>  ture or impulsive<br>  person<br>Need to insert prop-<br>  erly; learn and retain<br>  proper technique |
| IUD<br>  Copper | Once placed, effective<br>  for many months | Irregular bleeding<br>IUD may be lost with-<br>  out woman's knowl-<br>  edge<br>Some IUD's increase<br>  risk of pelvic inflam-<br>  matory disease<br>Increased risk of ecto-<br>  pic pregnancy |
| Medroxyprogesterone<br>  acetate (Depo-<br>  Provera), used wide-<br>  ly in many coun-<br>  tries; NOT AP-<br>  PROVED FOR THIS<br>  INDICATION BY<br>  FDA (Academy<br>  Statement, 1980) | Effective birth control<br>  for 3 months<br>Absence of menstrual<br>  bleeding | Not approved by FDA<br>Breakthrough bleeding |

mild mental retardation would be able to give informed consent, but that decisions for women with more severe mental retardation would have to be made by informed adults who are knowledgeable about the particular woman's circumstances and who make the decision according to the best interest of the woman. In 1984, 20 states had laws permitting review of sterilization requests. Protection of persons with mental retardation from unwanted pregnancies, sexual abuse, and sexually transmitted diseases, including AIDS, demands careful supervision of day-to-day activities.

In conclusion, there are various rewards in caring for children of parents with mental retardation: the pleasure of observing normal growth and development of children who were at risk for mental retardation, and the gratification and stimulation gained from working with other professionals in meeting an important social and medical challenge. Such efforts help provide children the "opportunity to achieve their full native potential."

## REFERENCES

Accardo, P.J., & Capute, A.J. (1979). *The pediatrician and the developmentally delayed child.* Baltimore: University Park Press.

American Academy of Pediatrics Committee on Drugs: *Medroxyprogesterone acetate (Depo-provera).* (1980). *Pediatrics, 65,* 648.

Behrman, R.E., & Vaughn, V.E. (1987). *Nelson textbook of pediatrics.* Philadelphia: W.B. Saunders.

Boodoosingh, L., & Brown, P. (1986). The culturally deprived child: Social and educational needs. *Psychiatric Clinics of North America, 9,* 767–776.

Chamberlain, A., Rauh, J., Passer, A., McGrath, M., & Burket, R. (1984). Fertility control for mentally retarded adolescents: 1. Sexual activity, sexual abuse, and contraception. *Pediatrics, 73*(4), 445–450.

Craft, A., & Craft, M. (1983). *Sex education and counseling for mentally handicapped people.* Baltimore: University Park Press.

De la Cruz, F., & LaVeck, G. (1973). *Human sexuality and the mentally retarded.* New York: Brunner/Mazel.

Farran, D.C., & McKinney, J.D. (1968). *Risk in intellectual and psychosocial development.* New York: Academic Press.

Feldman, M.A. (1986). Research on parenting mentally retarded persons. *Psychiatric Clinics of North America, 9,* 777–796.

Fisher, H., Krajicek, M., & Borthick, W. (1980). *Sex education for the developmentally disabled.* Baltimore: University Park Press.

Garber, H.L. (1988). *The Milwaukee project: Preventing mental retardation in children at risk.* Washington: American Association on Mental Retardation.

Goldstein, J., Freud, A., & Soluit, A. (1979). *Before the best interest of the child.* New York: Macmillan.

Hall, J.E. (1975). Sexuality and the mentally retarded. In R. Green (Ed.), *Human Sexuality: A Health Practitioner's Text (pp. 181–196).* Baltimore: Williams and Wilkins Co.

Passer, A., Rauh, J., Chamberlain, A., McGrath, M., & Burket, R. (1984). Fertility control for mentally retarded adolescents: II. Parental attitudes toward sterilization. *Pediatrics, 73*(4), 451–454.

Whitman, B.Y., Graves, B., & Accardo, P.J. (1987). Mentally retarded parents in the community: Identification method and needs assessment survey. *American Journal of Mental Deficiency, 91*(6), 636–638.

# V Legal and Ethical Issues

# 9 The Right to Marry for Persons with Mental Retardation

## Kathleen Marafino

> The drive to secure more legal rights for persons who are mentally retarded is still in an embryonic stage, but their rights to education, to employment, to live in the community, to bodily integrity, to adequate habilitation are now being asserted in the courts and before legislative and administrative bodies. One right of mentally retarded persons that is extremely important, but still incipient is the right to marry. (Shaman, 1978, pp. 61–62)

In 1978 when this statement was written, 37 states and the District of Columbia had statutes on the books that restricted or prohibited the right of persons with mental retardation to marry. Four other states (Shaman, 1978) had recently repealed their statutory limitations upon the right of persons with mental retardation to marry. Yet even in those four states with no statutory limitations upon the right to marry, there may be common law restrictions upon that right.

As people with mental retardation have exercised more fully their newly realized rights to live and work in the community, so too have they recognized the importance in their lives of the choice to marry (Shaman, 1978). The choice of marriage

149

offers people opportunities that may not be found outside of marriage. Marriage can provide a sense of acceptance and security. For persons with mental retardation who frequently face narrowed social opportunities, marriage can offer companionship and affection which is often lacking in their lives. Persons who have mental retardation have the same sexual desires and needs of any human being, and the marital relationship facilitates the opportunity for being sexually active. Simply stated, marriage is an important human right for all people.

## COMMON LAW THEORY OF MARRIAGE

The marriage relationship is generally considered a contractual relationship. It differs, however, from ordinary contracts in that it is a personal relationship over which the state exercises exclusive dominion (Corpus Juris Secundum, 1948, p. 806). The marriage contract is unique in that it cannot be revoked or dissolved by the parties themselves, but only by the sovereign power of the state. "Marriage is favored by the law and the public policy is to foster and protect marriage, to make it a permanent and public institution, to encourage the parties to live together, and to prevent separation" (Corpus Juris Secundum, 1948, p. 809). "In order to constitute a valid marriage, each party must be competent to contract marriage. [T]he general rule is that the test is the capacity of the person to understand the special nature of the contract of marriage, and the duties and responsibilities which it entails" (Corpus Juris Secundum, 1948 p. 820). A determination of competency to enter the marriage contract is to be based upon the facts and circumstances of each case. In some cases, the courts have used the capacity to contract generally as the standard. Other decisions have held that a *greater* or a *lesser* degree of capacity is required for the contract of marriage than for contracting generally. A person who has been formally adjudicated as incompetent is not necessarily incapable of contracting marriage. The court may inquire as to whether or not he or she has the specific mental capacity to understand the duties and responsibilities of marriage.

## ISSUES RAISED BY LEGAL
## RESTRICTIONS ON THE RIGHT TO MARRY

A number of issues that are generated from the prohibitions or limitations on marital status found in the majority of states' laws[1] are discussed in this section. First, the public policies upon which many of the restrictions on marriage are based are not fully supported by current data about persons with mental retardation. Second, the legal results of a prohibited marriage are varied without a reasonable or consistent basis for the variability. Third, the category of persons included within the coverage of the statutes is vague, imprecise, and sometimes inaccurate and archaic. Fourth, the application and interpretation of restrictive statutes is uneven, and most statutes contain no enforcement provisions. Fifth, the statutory restrictions have an impact upon fundamental constitutional rights and thereby constitute possible violations of the due process and equal protection clauses (Jacobs, 1977).

## 1.  Public Policies Underlying Legal Restrictions

Consideration will be given to the intended policy objectives of restricting the right to marry for persons with mental retardation. Each purpose will be reviewed for factual accuracy and constitutional adequacy.

   **A.   *To Protect Persons Who Have Mental Retardation***   Under the common law theory that marriage is a contract and that individuals need understanding and mental capacity to enter into the contract in order to validate it, states have enacted statutes prohibiting marriage by those who are mentally incompetent. The objective of such legislation was to protect persons with mental disabilities from entering into void contracts. As has often been true of protective legislation that is paternalistic in nature, it may work against and not for the persons intended to be protected. In the issue at hand, the protective statutes have worked to deny persons who have mental retardation their basic right to marry. The uniqueness of the marriage contract makes it unsuitable for strict adherence to all contract rules and denies persons with mental retardation, who are as capable as persons who do not have mental retardation of feeling and expressing love, the opportunity to do so in the context of marriage.

---

[1]See Appendix, "*Current Statutory Provisions Affecting the Right of Mentally Disabled Persons to Marry*" (The Right of . . . , 1977). At the time the appendix was compiled, 38 states and the District of Columbia prohibited or limited the right of persons with mental retardation to marry. Of those 39 jurisdictions, most of their statutes had been enacted within the preceding 10-year period. Many state statutes still contain archaic and offensive language (e.g., idiot and imbecile) in their provisions.

In addition, the common law contract theory requires that someone make a determination of capacity at the time the marriage contract is entered. Courts face the question of capacity after the fact and take into account the countervailing public policy supporting the presumption of the validity of a marriage.

**B.   To Prevent Procreation By Persons Who Have Mental Retardation (or To Protect the Public)**   The second policy underlying prohibitions against the marriage of persons with mental disabilities is the goal of preventing reproduction by persons whose children may become social and economic burdens to society, either because the parents would be incapable of supporting them and/or the children themselves would have mental retardation. This public policy, more recent than the common law contract policy, primarily prohibits marriage for eugenic[2] reasons and developed from the eugenics movement of the 1920s and 1930s. It is based on the theory that mental disability is hereditary and that the state has a duty to prevent procreation by persons who have mental retardation (Brakel, Parry, & Weiner, 1985). Eugenics theories formed the basis for the decision in the United States Supreme Court case of *Buck v. Bell* (1927), in which Justice Holmes made his infamous statement, "[t]hree generations of imbeciles are enough."

The eugenics rationale is obvious in those statutes that allow, for example, exceptions to the marriage prohibition if the person with mental retardation has been sterilized or when a female who has mental retardation is over the age of 45 or if a man with mental retardation is marrying a woman who is over 45. As of 1985, only three statutes still contained such provisions (Brakel et al., 1985). A more humane approach to persons with mental retardation, recognizing the intrinsic value of individuals with mental disabilities, has contributed to the decline of the eugenics movement.

Eugenics theories are not supported by available scientific data. Thus, statutes that limit or prohibit marriage for eugenic considerations do so without scientific or factual basis. Modern scientific data demonstrate that not all kinds of mental retardation are hereditary. Mental retardation may be caused by purely genetic factors, by genetic factors in combination with environmental factors, by purely environmental factors,

---

[2]"Eugenic" literally means well-born, relating to the bearing of sound offspring. Eugenics is defined as the movement devoted to improving the human species through the control of hereditary factors in mating (Webster's New World Dictionary 482 [2d ed., 1980]).

by injury, or by deprivation. Eighty to 90 percent of all persons with mental retardation have parents who do not have mental retardation. Thus, it is grossly underinclusive and over-inclusive to prohibit persons with mental retardation from marrying, as a means of preventing the procreation of children who have mental retardation. Restricting marriage by persons with mental retardation does not prevent them from having children. Not only is the marriage prohibition unduly burdensome as a method of birth control, it is not effective.

C.  *To Disallow Unfit Spouses*  A seemingly more benign reason for restricting the right to marry is the belief that persons with mental retardation are unfit to be spouses. One response to that theory is that the issue of determining spousal fitness is not a legitimate state interest. Certainly, fitness is not a prerequisite for marriage by persons who do not have mental retardation. Moreover, the belief that persons with mental retardation are unfit spouses is very likely derived from assumptions about these persons that are unsubstantiated scientifically. This approach also fails to account for the range and variability in intellectual capacity and other skills among persons with mental retardation. The prohibition on marriage is both an imperfect and unreasonable limitation on the rights of these individuals.

In summary, even today much of the public policy upon which prohibitory statutes are based treats people with mental retardation as a homogenous class without regard for individual differences. It represents a still paternalistic and unenlightened view of persons with mental retardation. Legislative restrictions upon marriage should take into account the abilities and needs of persons with mental retardation from a modern perspective founded on well-documented factual data.

## 2.  Legal Results of Prohibited Marriages

Varying legal consequences, often unclear and inconsistent, result from the prohibitions on the marriage of person(s) with mental retardation. Modern statutes, in a minority of jurisdictions, follow the common law rule and declare the marriage void ab initio (i.e., from the beginning) if either party is incapable of understanding the nature of the marriage contract. The legal consequence of a void marriage is that the validity of the marriage may be attacked directly by the parties as well as collaterally by third parties. If a marriage is declared void, it has an impact on the property rights of the parties and may impose serious economic hardship on the putative spouse.[3] It may also raise a question about the legitimacy of children born of the union. (About half of the states provide for legitimizing the children of a void marriage. See Brakel et al., 1985.) Some statutes declare that, even though marriage with a person who has mental retardation is void, or annulled, it must be so declared by a court of competent jurisdiction.

The majority of states' statutes deem a prohibited marriage to be voidable with varying approaches used regarding proving incapacity. Generally the laws impose the burden of proving incapacity, at the time the marriage was contracted, upon the person seeking to invalidate the marriage. Questions arise over the person(s) who may have standing to bring an annulment action. In some states, only the mentally disabled person or his or her guardian may bring the proceedings. Other states view it as a strictly personal right, with the action available only to the disabled person. That approach can create a dilemma. The mentally disabled person may be disallowed from bringing the action by virtue of the disability and at the same time be incompetent to give his or her consent to another person to act on his or her behalf (Jacobs, 1977). Other variations allow only the nondisabled spouse to bring the action and, in some statutes, no provision is made regarding standing in an annulment proceeding.

Thus, a prohibited marriage can result in varied legal consequences with respect to the status of the marriage. The outcomes may be confusing at best and often fail to reflect clearly the public policy underlying the prohibition.

## 3.  Categories of Persons Prohibited From Marrying

Very few statutes clearly define the individuals for whom marriage is prohibited. The categories of persons prohibited from marriage seem to include those with all degrees of mental disability. The descriptions of persons prohibited from marriage that seem to include those with mental retardation are: imbecile, idiot, persons under conservatorship or guardianship, persons of unsound mind, mental retardate, mentally disabled,

---

[3]"Putative marriage" means a marriage contracted in good faith and in ignorance (on one or both sides) so that impediments exist which render it unlawful (Black's Law Dictionary 1402 [4th ed., 1968]).

mentally retarded, feebleminded, mental deficiency, weak-minded, and institutionalized persons (Brakel et al., 1985). The North Dakota statute is drawn more narrowly by limiting the coverage of the statute to those "institutionalized as severely retarded" (Brakel et al., 1985).

A desired objective in writing laws is to put the ordinary citizen on notice as to what is allowed or prohibited under that law. Where that is not or cannot be easily accomplished, at the very least, those charged with implementing the statute (e.g., issuing clerks and clergypersons) should be provided with specific guidelines to assist them in exercising the discretion granted them.

While calling for greater clarity and specificity in identifying the persons whose right to marry is limited or restricted, it is desirable also that the identified categories be carefully delineated to include only those persons for whom sound public policy dictates such an infringement on their rights.

## 4.  Statutory Enforcement

The right of the state to regulate marriage and divorce was long ago endorsed by the United States Supreme Court (*Fensterwald v. Burk*, 1918) as a proper exercise of the state's police power (police power means the authority of the State to regulate matters pertaining to public health, welfare and safety). State enforcement of statutes prohibiting marriage of persons with mental disabilities has taken a number of forms. In some states, proof of the absence of incompetency is required. Others leave the determination of capacity to understand the contract of marriage to the discretion of the clerk charged with issuing marriage licenses. Still others merely establish penalties, fines and/or imprisonment, directed either at the mentally disabled person applying for the license, the issuing clerk, the solemnizing clergyperson, or the nondisabled applicant. Only 10 states have established enforcement mechanisms (Brakel et al., 1985); those statutes typically provide for a fine or brief imprisonment. In the absence of a requirement that applicants for a marriage license affirmatively provide evidence of mental capacity, it is difficult for the state to identify instances in which an applicant lacks mental capacity. In states that do not prohibit marriage, but provide for annulment or divorce on the grounds of mental disability, neither deterrence from marriage nor effective application of the law results (Brakel et al., 1985).

## 5.  Protection of Fundamental Constitutional Rights

*A.  Equal Protection*  Statutes that limit or prohibit the right of persons with mental retardation to marry are subject to constitutional attack under the equal protection clause of the Fourteenth Amendment of the Constitution of the United States ("no State shall make or enforce any law which shall abridge the privileges or immunities of citizens of the United States; nor shall any State deprive any person of life, liberty, or property, without due process of law; nor deny to any person within its jurisdiction the equal protection of the laws"). A long line of cases support the proposition that the right to marry and procreate are fundamental interests subject to strict judicial scrutiny. Supreme Court decisions have established the individual's right to marry, right to privacy, and the integrity of the family unit (e.g., *Griswold v. Connecticut,* 1965; *Loving v. Virginia,* 1967; *Stanley v. Illinois,* 1972). States must set forth a compelling reason for restricting a fundamental constitutional right. Even if some logical reasons exist for limiting in some fashion the right to marry for some persons with mental retardation, that does not justify discrimination against an entire class of persons. While the suitability of a person with mental retardation as a spouse may not have been conclusively established by scientific evidence, neither has that suitability been proven for other recognizable groups who may be high-risk spouses (e.g., alcoholics, drug addicts, physically abusive persons). The state has not restricted the right to marry for those groups.

Those statutes that limit the right to marry by imposing sterilization as a precondition impinge upon two fundamental interests, the right to marry and the right to procreate. The decision in *Skinner v. Oklahoma* (1942) raises questions about the constitutionality of laws requiring that persons with mental retardation be sterilized before they may marry. Such a requirement would in all probability not meet even the minimum level of scrutiny under equal protection, since the statutory provision is not reasonably related to the purpose it intends to achieve. A statute imposing a sterilization requirement fails to achieve its intended purpose because it applies to persons whose mental retardation is not hereditary.

The Supreme Court in *Stanley* made the point that, while procedure by presumption is always cheaper and easier than individual determination, it is constitutionally unacceptable when fundamental individual rights are ignored. Under the

*Stanley* Court analysis, a presumption that all people with mental retardation are unsuitable for marriage fails to meet constitutional standards of acceptability. Statutes prohibiting marriage of persons with mental retardation should set forth a permissible state objective to justify the abridgement of a fundamental right. That state objective can then be considered and evaluated in light of the individual circumstances of each case.

**B.  Substantive Due Process**  Statutes may be constitutionally infirm for overbreadth. In order to withstand constitutional scrutiny, the classifications of persons restricted in the right to marry should be precise in describing persons included in the statute's coverage and narrow enough to be supported by sound public policy and scientific evidence. The provisions should focus specifically on the capacity to understand and undertake the responsibilities of the marriage relationship. Nebraska enacted a statute that does specify incompetence to enter into the marriage contract (Nebraska Revised Statutes, 1978). Even that approach may require additional specifications to avoid the risk of circular reasoning.

Overall, the avowed purposes for prohibiting marriage of persons with mental retardation are both overbroad and underinclusive in scope. Such deficiencies would make many states' statutes vulnerable to constitutional attack.

**C.  Procedural Due Process**  Under the due process clause of the Fourteenth Amendment "a person may not be deprived of his life, liberty or property without due process of law." The fundamentals of procedural due process include a hearing before an impartial decision-maker after notice is provided and an opportunity to present one's own case. In *J.L. v. Parham*, (1979) the federal District Court held that "where the state undertakes to act in parens patriae, it has the inescapable duty to vouchsafe due process." The District Court stated further that the deprivation of liberty concerns not only the liberty that includes freedom from bodily restraint, but also the freedom to live a normal American life. Surely that freedom includes the choice of a normal married life. Statutes must provide procedural safeguards that ensure individual adjudication of competency by a neutral judicial officer, not a clerk granted unlimited discretion.

There are relatively few reported cases dealing with the denial of marriage licenses because of mental disability. Thus, little data are available to illustrate the effect that the application of restrictive statutes has on persons with mental retardation seeking to assert their right to marry. Perhaps persons who are denied licenses simply have not had the legal assistance they needed to appeal a license denial. In one reported case (Application for F.A. marriage license, 1955), the court set forth three criteria that would affect its decision regarding the issuance of a license: 1) a determination that full disclosure of the medical history of the person with a mental disability has been made to both parties, 2) that the court is satisfied that the applicant with a disability is stable enough to adjust to the normal pressures of marriage, and 3) that there is a reasonable expectation that offspring of such a marriage will be normal and healthy and raised in a proper environment. These criteria raise constitutional issues with respect to equal protection as well as due process claims.

## PROPOSALS FOR
## STATUTORY REFORM AND POLICY FORMULATION

If states choose to continue to restrict in any way the right of persons with mental retardation to marry, then certain matters of statutory revision should be addressed. Initially, the state should formulate and the statute should reflect a legitimate and clearly stated public policy. The policy should be premised on the recognition of the intrinsic worth of persons with mental retardation and should acknowledge all of their human needs and abilities. Second, the language of the statute must be precise and correlate closely with the expressed public policy. The restrictions on the fundamental right to marry should be no broader than necessary to serve the public policy, nor should they, where a limitation is imposed, exceed the scope of restriction necessary to achieve the goal of the policy. Moreover, persons affected by the statutory limitations should be able to be identified with a high degree of reliability.

Procedural safeguards must be incorporated into the statute to ensure that each individual is provided the opportunity for a hearing and other measures traditionally designed to comport with the requirements of due process. Some authorities suggest removing the void-voidable designations and retaining only the voidable designation. Uniformity from state to state would be desirable. Another reform suggested is to enact a statute of limitations on bringing annulment actions (see Jacobs, 1977).

Public policy formulation regarding the right to marry for persons with mental retardation introduces a complex array of issues. Other legal and practical matters involving the right to procreate, the right not to procreate, and the right to the custody and care of one's children affect the right to marry and the development of new policies. Public policy analysis surrounding restrictions upon the right to marry should take into account the full range and complexity of these interrelated issues.

Some of the public policies underlying past and present statutes do not provide a satisfactory basis for modern policy formulation. For example, while unfitness as a spouse may represent a reasonable concern for some people with mental retardation, the presumption that all persons with mental retardation would be unfit spouses is unacceptable. As discussed earlier, such a presumption is both overbroad with respect to persons with mental retardation and underinclusive for failure to include other categories of potentially unfit spouses.

Another historical policy for prohibiting marriage discussed earlier was to prevent procreation. If reconsidered, that policy would have to be narrowed to include only those for whom procreation was a real possibility and for whom the mental retardation was hereditary. Discouraging persons who might be unfit parents from marriage could be another reason for this policy. The objective of avoiding unfit parents would suffer also from overbreadth and underinclusivity. Moreover, the concern for adequacy of parenting and the measurement thereof should be determined by explicit statement and assessment of functional parenting skills.

There is also the policy of protecting persons with mental retardation from entering void marriage contracts. That purported goal could be easily fulfilled by revising statutes to eliminate the legal consequence of void marriages of individuals with mental disabilities.

An additional policy that could be advanced would be to protect the children who might be born of the marriage. Many of the same considerations apply here that were mentioned with respect to the goal of preventing procreation. Less drastic alternatives, such as birth control short of sterilization, could be used to serve this policy. Birth control and sterilization do not, of course, fully address the concerns regarding marriage of persons with mental retardation and, in fact, open up many of the same dilemmas in the context of other legal rights.

A policy that might be constitutionally supportable would be that of preventing the imposition of marital responsibilities on those persons incapable of understanding the nature and obligations of the marriage relationship. The application of such a policy would require that there be a formal adjudication of an individual's mental capacity to enter into the marriage relationship. In order to assess that specific capacity, there would need to be clear identification, in behavioral terms, of the obligations assumed by marrying and individual evaluation on the basis of identified skills. A process similar to or in conjunction with limited guardianship could be employed. This suggested policy would require further development, however, to address the issue of enforcement.

New solutions may need to be created in an attempt to resolve or reconcile some of the competing interests of the person with mental retardation, the prospective spouse whether disabled or nondisabled, children who may be born of the union, and society. Possibly the concept of "supported marriage" could be explored. Some individuals who could benefit from marriage, but who do not have the mental capacity to appreciate fully the obligations of marriage, could choose to marry if supportive services and semi-independent alternatives were created. Existing services, such as residential placement, could be expanded to include married couples.

## CONCLUSION

Marriage is an essential human relationship as well as a fundamental legal right. Denying that right and opportunity to all persons with mental retardation cannot be justified. Persons with mental retardation vary greatly in individual abilities, intellectual and otherwise. There is a wide spectrum of ability among persons with mental retardation as there is among persons who do not have mental retardation. The state should not restrict the right to marry based on stereotypical notions and inaccurate information. Available data do not support the presumption that all persons with mental retardation are less capable than persons who do not have mental retardation of functioning successfully as spouses. It is reasonable to expect that many individuals who have mental retardation will succeed in marriage as they have in other areas (e.g., community living and employment) when allowed the opportunity. Prohibiting or restricting the opportunity to marry denies individuals the right to make their own choices and assume their own risks.

Past experiences have shown us that lack of expectations or low expectations are often self-fulfilling prophecies.

## REFERENCES

Application for F.A. marriage license, 4 Pa. D. & C. 2d 1, 5 Pa. Fiduc. 561 (1955).

Jacobs, L. (1977). The right of the mentally disabled to marry: A statutory evaluation. *Journal of Family Law, 15,* 463, 464, 470, 485, Appendix.

Brakel, S., Parry, J., & Weiner, B. (1985). *The mentally disabled and the law* (3rd ed.). Chicago: American Bar Foundation. 507, 509.

Buck v. Bell, 274 U.S. 200, 207 (1927).

*Corpus Juris Secundum* (Vol. 55). (1948). St. Paul, MN: West Publishing Co.

Fensterwald v. Buck, 129 Md. 131, 98 A. 358, reh. denied, 248 U.S. 592 (1918).

Griswold v. Connecticut, 381 U.S. 479 (1965).

J.L. v. Parham, 422 U.S. 584 (1979); 412 F. Supp. 112, 136, 138 (M.D. Ga. 1976).

Loving v. Virginia, 388 U.S. 1 (1967).

Neb. Rev. Stat. § 42-107 (1978).

Shaman, J. (1978). Persons who are mentally retarded: Their right to marry and have children. *Family Law Quarterly, 12,* 61, 62, 65.

Skinner v. Oklahoma, 316 U.S. 535 (1942).

Stanley v. Illinois, 405 U.S. 645, 657 (1972).

# 10 | Parental Rights of Persons with Mental Retardation

Kathleen Marafino

## I. INTRODUCTION

Chapter 10 explores the law governing parents' rights with respect to their children. It is critical that the reader appreciate first the overall legal context of the issues of parental rights before trying to evaluate the manner in which the legal system treats parents who have mental retardation. Initially, consideration will be given to the extent to which parents in general are protected by the law from State interference with their right to the custody and care of their children. The protections afforded parents are derived from the United States Constitution as well as state statutes and case law. Parental rights must be considered in the context of the rights afforded to children and also the State's dual interests in assuring the well-being of children and encouraging family stability. Next, an analysis will be made of how the legal system has treated parents who have mental retardation. Consideration will be given to those circumstances in which mental retardation forms the basis for or contributes to the decision to limit or sever parental rights. Other factors that could occur in conjunction with mental retardation and may even be likely to occur will not be independently considered (e.g., indigence, substance abuse, incarceration/commitment, mental illness). It should be noted, however, that these factors occur with some regularity in the reported cases dealing with the termination of the rights of parents who have mental retardation. The review of case law will focus almost exclusively on cases where the parent with mental retardation is living in the community, not in an institution.

## II.  PARENTS' RIGHT TO CUSTODY
## AND CONTROL OF CHILDREN—A HISTORICAL OVERVIEW

Traditionally, parents have been granted broad rights to the custody and control of their children, and courts have accorded great deference to that parental right (Minnesota adopts a best interests standard in parental rights termination proceedings: In re J. J. B. [hereinafter cited as Minnesota adopts . . .], 1987). Proceeding from the premise that the biological parents are the legal and appropriate custodians, society has had to fashion a remedy to the problem of inadequate parenting, whether it be abuse, neglect, or abandonment. Approaches to the problem of deficient parenting during colonial times included punishing child abusers under the criminal law, an approach that caused the child financial hardship along with the emotional trauma already inflicted upon him or her (Parental rights termination: Are the interests of parents, children, and the state mutually exclusive [hereinafter cited as Parental rights . . . ], 1987). Another approach from that era was removal of the child from the natural home for his or her protection and placement in an institution. This intervention, aimed at protecting the child versus punishing the parent, also placed an additional burden on the child, that of separation from the family.

Recognition of the detrimental effects that these approaches had on children led to the development of new modes of intervention. "The modern approach recognizes the value of preserving the family unit, and therefore the goal is to 'rehabilitate' the family by treating the causes of abuse or neglect rather than their effects" (Parental rights. . . , 1987, p. 299). The current preferred method is to use temporary removal of the child from the natural home when necessary for the child's protection. During the period of separation, social service agencies may develop a rehabilitation plan for the family with services provided to the parents to enable them to become adequate caregivers. The goal of the rehabilitation plan is the reunification of the family.

When a decision is made, either by the parents or the State, that the child should be removed permanently from the natural home, then the issues of adoption and termination of parental rights are raised. In both England and the United States adoption is governed by statute; the earliest in the United States was enacted in Massachusetts in 1851 (Brakel et al., 1985, p. 516). In the early adoption statutes, consent by the parents was required except where the parents neglected, abused, or abandoned their children (Brakel, Parry, & Weiner, 1985). Similarly, state statutes today uniformly require parental consent prior to adoption, unless the conduct of the parent(s) has threatened the child's well-being (Brakel et al., 1985). In that circumstance, the child welfare and legal systems become involved in a termination of parental rights proceeding rather than a consensual adoption process. An additional exception to the requirement of parental consent to adoption has been created in recent times when the biological parents are mentally disabled (Brakel et al., 1985).

## III.  CONSTITUTIONAL PROTECTION OF PARENTAL RIGHTS

Traditionally, great deference has been given to parental rights, based upon the presumption that parents will provide better care for the child than could the State. The constitutional rights of custody to one's child and family integrity are recognized by a line of United States Supreme Court decisions as fundamental liberty interests under the due process clause of the Fourteenth Amendment. In *Stanley v. Illinois*, the Supreme Court recognized the "essential right to conceive and raise one's children." One court, describing the development of constitutional law since *Stanley v. Illinois*, acknowledged a "due process evolution that has taken place in the area of parental rights" (*In re Montgomery*, 1984). Further strengthening of parental rights came about with the case of *Santosky v. Kramer* (1982) "in which the Court held that the due process right of parents required petitioners [the agency of the state petitioning for termination of parental rights] to prove grounds for termination of parental rights by clear and convincing evidence.[1]" The fundamental liberty interest in maintaining the family unit, recognized in the *Santosky* case, is an interest shared by parent and child. The Court in *Santosky* stated also that parents have a fundamental liberty interest in the care, custody, and management of their children. Thus, the State's interference with the parent-child relationship, historically exercised in cases of neglect, abuse, and abandonment, is now limited constitutionally. According the status of fundamental rights to parents' interests imposes upon the State the burden of justifying by clear and convincing evidence its interference with those rights.

## IV. CHILDREN'S RIGHTS

Historically, few legal rights have been conferred upon children, in contrast to their parents. "At one time children were regarded as mere chattel over which parents were able to exercise total control" (Parental rights . . . , 1987, p. 300). As mentioned above, children share with their parents a legal interest in the integrity of the family unit. Since a child lacks the capacity and maturity to act in his or her own best interests, the law generally presumes that parental custody serves the child's best interests (Comment: Parental rights in emotional . . . [cited in Minnesota adopts . . . , 1987]; Hershkowitz, 1985 [cited in Minnesota adopts . . . , 1987]; Minnesota adopts . . . , 1987; *Parham v. J. R.,* 1979). The enactment of termination statutes by state legislatures may be viewed as evidence of a legislative intent to limit parental control and consequently as a recognition of certain basic rights for children, including the child's right to a safe home. (Hayes & Morse, 1982 [cited in Minnesota adopts . . . , 1987]; Minnesota adopts . . . , 1987; Parental rights . . . , 1987; Termination of . . . , 1977–78). Recognition of the rights of children reached new levels in the early 1970s with the introduction of the concept of the "best interests of the child" prevailing over consideration of parental fitness in some cases (Goldstein, Freud, & Solnit [cited in Parental rights . . . , 1987]; Parental rights . . . , 1987).

---

[1]This intermediate standard of proof imposes upon the petitioners the burden of producing more evidence than required under the traditional civil standard of "mere preponderance of evidence." Yet the clear and convincing standard is less demanding than the criminal standard of proof "beyond a reasonable doubt" (*Santosky v. Kramer,* 1982).

## V.  STATE INTERESTS

The State has dual interests in protecting children and promoting family integrity. Its legitimate interest in protecting children derives from its parens patriae power.[2]

"Every state has made some statutory provision whereby the state can step in to protect the health, safety, and well-being of its infant citizens from endangerment by abusive, neglectful, or simply unavailable parents" (22 A.L.R., 1983, p. 778). As part of its protective role with respect to children the State has an interest in ensuring that children have the opportunity to live in a safe and stable environment. In circumstances where the maintenance of the family unit presents a threat to the child's well-being, the State's interest in the protection of the child generally prevails over its interest in family integrity. When the State deems it necessary to intervene in the family relationship, it may do so either by seeking a change of custody from the biological parent(s) on a temporary basis or by seeking to sever permanently the parent-child relationship. Generally, state interference is warranted only in cases of parental unfitness, and the contours of that power to interfere are limited by the parent's constitutional rights. "Temporary removal of children from their homes has been a practice for some time, but permanent severance of parental rights is relatively new" (Comment: Termination of . . . , 1986 [cited in Parental rights . . . , 1987]; Parental rights . . . , 1987, p. 300). When seeking termination of parental rights, the State must establish parental unfitness, the risk of actual or probable harm to the child if he or she remains in the parent's custody, and the probability that the conditions placing the child at risk will persist (Brakel et al., 1985, p. 517).

## VI.  STATE INTERVENTION IN PARENTAL RIGHTS

### A.  Overview

In every state, child neglect statutes protect children from persistent inadequate care. These laws typically allow the state to intervene in the parent-child relationship to safeguard the "best

---

[2]*Parens patriae* literally means "parent of the country." *Black's Law Dictionary* 100 (5th ed., 1979). See Minnesota adopts. . .(1987, p. 1267 nn. 28 & 29) for cases and authorities discussing the parens patriae doctrine.

interests of the child" and to protect the child from physical or mental harm. State administrative agencies investigate suspected neglect and petition for a judicial hearing when they determine that legal action is necessary. The statutes authorize temporary severance of the parent-child relationship when the court finds parental neglect and permanent termination of parental rights if the neglect is particularly serious or longstanding. (Retarded parents in neglect proceedings: The erroneous assumption of parental inadequacy [hereinafter cited as Retarded parents . . .], 1979, p. 785)

## B.  Initial State Intervention and Temporary Removal of Children

Every state has enacted legislation that enables the State to intervene on behalf of children whose health and safety may be jeopardized by parental custody. The child may be removed temporarily from the natural home with the possibility of eventual return. Even where the State intervenes only to the extent of temporary removal of the child, the parents still retain their interest in the right of family integrity. The State may be required to provide assistance to the parents during the time the child is removed from the home in an attempt to enable the parents to provide adequate care for the child upon return.

State intervention begins when a petition is filed by an agency or individual alleging that a child is being abused, neglected, or somehow is in need of protection (Areen, 1975 [cited in Parental rights. . . , 1987]). A court will then conduct a hearing to determine whether in fact the child is dependent[3] and in need of protective intervention. If the complaint is found to be valid, the court may award custody of the child to the State or some other foster care provider with the court continuing its jurisdiction over the case.

> Once the court assumes jurisdiction in a case of child dependency there is a very high probability that the child will be removed from the home for at least some period of time. Furthermore, statistics from 1975 demonstrate that once a child is removed, it is likely that he will never return home. The entire system has been criticized, most notably by Michael Wald, as being unnecessarily harmful to both children and parents. Wald found fault with "extremely broad and vague" statutes that authorized state intervention in the first place. He pointed out that these statutes focused on parental behavior rather than on "specific harm to the child." As Wald said, [t]ermination is the last act in a production that begins by labeling a child (dependent)." This

---

[3]Under a statute relating to dependent children, "dependent" is synonymous with "neglected." *Black's Law Dictionary* 525 (4th ed., 1968).

being so, he advocated that termination standards should be related for both removal and return of children in order to achieve a coordinated system of intervention. (Wald, 1975, p. 985 [cited in Parental rights. . . , 1987, p. 302])

Although removal of custody, even temporarily, impinges upon a fundamental parental right, the legal standards and safeguards accompanying such intervention are less stringent than in termination actions. Traditional due process requirements (e.g., rights to notice, hearing, representation, production of evidence, confrontation of witnesses) are relevant, however, even with this lesser degree of state intervention.

## C.  Termination of Parental Rights

The State may go further and seek to remove the child permanently from the natural home and make the child available for adoption by another family. In order to free children for adoption without having parental consent, the State initiates proceedings to terminate parental rights. The public policy served by termination actions is that of providing dependent children with the opportunity for a secure and stable home setting at as young an age as possible. "The permanency and stability envisioned by the statute are largely illusory, however, because relatively few children removed from their parents ever get adopted" (Termination of parental rights—suggested reforms and responses [hereinafter cited as Termination of . . .], 1985, p. 1177). If children then become victims of "foster care drift," then "one might reasonably ask how often termination orders actually are in the children's best interests" (Termination of. . . , 1985, p. 1183).

The courts face the challenge of weighing and balancing the interests of the child and possible threats to the child's welfare with the parent's rights to custody and family integrity and the potential severance of those rights. (455 U.S. 745, 747–748 [1982]).[4] In addition to considering the parent's interest in determining how his or her child will be raised and the child's interest in a stable and healthy environment, the court must address the State's sometimes conflicting interests in the protection of the child and family autonomy.

---

[4]The court in *Santosky v. Kramer* (1982) said that the following three interests must be balanced in termination proceedings: the private interests of the parents and children; the risk of error contained in the state termination procedure; and the state interest in the use of the procedure.

Termination statutes have been challenged as violations of constitutional rights to due process and equal protection of the law. Fundamental constitutional rights can be abridged only to serve a compelling state interest. "Temporary removal of children from their homes has been a practice for some time, but permanent severance of parental rights is relatively new" (Parental rights. . . , 1987, p. 300). The parent faced with a termination proceeding is assured of due process rights including a hearing on his or her fitness to continue to care for the child and proof of unfitness by clear and convincing evidence. Any statutory presumption of unfitness must bear a substantial relationship to the fact shown, and the parent must be provided the opportunity to rebut any presumption. The statute itself must be sufficiently clear so that a person of ordinary intelligence could understand its meaning and conform his or her conduct thereto (22 A.L.R., 1983).

The Supreme Court in *Santosky* noted that both parent and child "share an interest in avoiding erroneous termination" (455 U.S. 745, 765 [1982]). The Court further stated that "[e]ven when a child's natural home is imperfect, permanent removal from that home will not necessarily improve his welfare" (455 U.S. 765n.15).

During the 1970s and 1980s, termination statutes were amended in response to deficiencies in social service systems[5] as well as in response to constitutional requirements such as those set out in *Santosky*. The changes included: 1) providing more specific grounds for termination to avoid claims of violating due process for vagueness; 2) requiring a showing of harmful effect on the child, not simply evidence of parental misconduct; 3) ensuring that notice is provided to parents; 4) developing remedial plans to increase the skills of parents whose children have been found dependent; and 5) setting time frames for accomplishing the goals of the rehabilitation plan.

In 1980, the state trend toward rehabilitation of troubled families was encouraged by Congress when it enacted a federal statute that "provided fiscal incentives to states to emphasize the goals of prevention and reunification" (Adoption Assistance and Child Welfare Act, 1980). Among other things, the act required case plans and case reviews to further the goal of family reunification.

---

[5]"Children in foster care tend to bounce from one placement to another, a phenomenon known as 'foster care drift'" (Termination of. . ., 1985, p. 1183 [citing Garrison, 1983, p. 426]).

## D. Standards of Proof in Termination Proceedings

The two most common standards used by state courts in termination proceedings are the parental fitness standard and the child's best interests standard. The standards differ primarily in the weight they give to the competing interests involved. The parental fitness standard emphasizes the parent's fundamental right to custody. The child's best interests standard focuses on the child's need. Parent and child obviously share an interest in maintaining the family unit.

The parental fitness standard is based on the common law presumption, supported by Supreme Court decisions (*Ginsberg v. New York*, 1968; *Meyer v. Nebraska*, 1923; *Moore v. City of Cleveland*, 1977; *Quilloin v. Walcott*, 1978; *Santosky v. Kramer*, 1982; *Smith v. Organization of Foster Families*, 1977; *Stanley v. Illinois*, 1972), that parents act in their child's best interests and have the fundamental right to custody. States adopting this standard terminate parental rights only after a finding of unfitness and, in close cases, generally find in favor of parental custody. Usually statutes set out specific factors to be considered in determining fitness or unfitness so that the standard can be applied with relative ease.

The best interests standard also considers parental fitness but not as the sole determining factor. Statutes adopting the best interests standard usually do not specify the factors that must be considered. Greater flexibility can be achieved with this standard but with flexibility come the risks of vagueness, arbitrariness, and inconsistent application.

Some jurisdictions apply the best interests standard by considering the child's best interests in conjunction with parental fitness. Both standards are applied with the child's best interests being the predominate consideration. Other states, such as Wisconsin, use a bifurcated hearing approach and allow consideration of the best interests of the child only after a finding of parental unfitness.

As previously noted, many statutes employing the best interests standard lack specificity. Of the state statutes that do enumerate factors to evaluate when applying this standard, some do so with broad provisions such as the "child's physical and emotional needs" and others with more defined factors such as: the child's need for a stable home, the child's attachment to biological or foster parents, length of the child's separation from biological parents, and the child's ability to integrate into a substitute home. Still other statutes provide no guidelines for interpreting and applying the best interests standard (Minnesota adopts . . , 1987). One commentator, Gloria Christopherson, recently expressed concern that inconsistent decisions will inevitably follow unless the substantive factors comprising a child's best interests are clearly indicated by legislatures (Minnesota adopts . . . , 1987).

> The circumstances of many parents involved in termination proceedings make value judgments likely. Many parents involved in termination proceedings are chemically dependent; some parents are mentally retarded; some parents are mentally ill; and a disproportionate share of dependent or neglected children are minorities. (Minnesota adopts . . . , 1987) In addition to the judge's values, parents, custodians, legislatures, social service agencies, guardians ad litem, and children themselves all have different opinions on what constitutes the child's best interests. (Minnesota adopts . . . , 1987)

Unless specific substantive and procedural guidelines are established, there is little likelihood that consistent, value-neutral applications of the law will occur. Consequently, terminations could occur in some instances where they are not warranted and fail to occur in circumstances where they are genuinely warranted.

Christopherson advocates for the explicit adoption of the best interests standard because, in her opinion, if clearly specified factors are incorporated into the legislation, then the best interests standard is the approach best able to serve the competing interests of the parent, the child, and the State. It also holds the potential for leading to more consistent, less value-laden judgments in termination cases (Minnesota adopts . . . , 1987).

## VII. STATE INTERVENTION WHEN THE PARENT(S) HAVE MENTAL RETARDATION

The preceding discussion of parental rights and state intervention also applies to cases in which the parents have mental retardation. In this section, issues that are more specific to parents with mental retardation will be reviewed. Legislatures and courts have paid considerable attention, during the 1980s, to the rights of parents with mental disabilities.

## A. Temporary Removal of Custody from Parent with Mental Retardation

In an action to remove custody of the child from a parent who has mental retardation, the parent's mental capacity will generally be addressed by the courts.

> State statutory law of custody today uniformly defers to the best interest of the child and where it is modeled after the Uniform Marriage and Divorce Act as it is in many states, the law provides that a determination of this interest shall include consideration of the "mental and physical health of all individuals involved." (Brakel et al., 1985, p. 516)

Taking into consideration the parent's mental health does not, however, yield consistent outcomes in the treatment of parents with mental disabilities. In *Price v. Price* (1979) the court refused to transfer custody from the mother who had mental retardation to the father when it stated that incompetence to rear children cannot be inferred merely from the fact of general mental or even legal incapacity (Brakel et al., 1985). An opposite result was reached in *In re C.L.M.* (1981). Evidence of the mother's general incapacity supported a custody change to the State based on the potential for harm or neglect of the child.

## B. Nonconsensual Adoption

In the early statutes, the only time that parental consent to adoption was not required was when there was parental misconduct such as abandonment, neglect, or cruelty. Later, nonconsensual adoptions were extended to cases where the parents have mental disabilities. That exception has been allowed probably because of the view that persons with mental disabilities are incapable of consenting to the adoption of their children (Brakel et al., 1985, p. 517).

In some circumstances, parents who have mental retardation may be willing to have their children adopted but, because of their mental incapacity, may not be able to give valid legal consent. Brakel, a noted authority in the field of mental disability law, argues that statutes should clearly distinguish between the circumstance in which the primary issue is valid consent and the termination case in which consent is not even considered. In the termination action, parental fitness, as opposed to consent, is the matter under consideration.

According to Brakel, "The distinction is often obscured in the literature on the subject, as it is in statutory provisions." Statutes in about half of the states now do distinguish between nonconsensual adoption and termination of parental rights. "The remaining states, however, operate with only one provision whose objective is unclear and whose suitability for addressing either one or both situations is often ambiguous (Brakel et al., 1985, p. 517).

Brakel asserts that the issues of nonconsensual adoption and termination can be separated. In the adoption case where parents want to give consent but are mentally incapable of doing so, courts should demand evidence sufficient to support a formal adjudication of incompetence, specifically incompetence to decide to relinquish the right to one's child. In termination proceedings, where consent is not an issue, then no finding of incapacity is necessary.

## C.  Termination of Parental Rights Proceedings

*1.  Recent Developments in the Law*  During the 1980s, there was considerable litigation relating to adoption and termination cases involving parents with mental disabilities. The procedural and substantive rights of parents with mental retardation have been addressed by the courts (Brakel et al., 1985). Many statutes have therefore been interpreted and applied by the courts and there is now a significant body of case law.

Thus, courts are confronting with new frequency the question of the competency of people with mental retardation to raise their own children (Retarded parents . . . , 1979). In the mid-1970s, there was a substantial increase in the number of child neglect cases involving parents with mental retardation. That increase was due in part to the repeal of involuntary sterilization statutes and possibly to the greater availability of legal assistance to persons with mental retardation (Retarded parents . . . , 1979). Continued activity in this area of the law might be expected because of further limitations on access to sterilization. Moreover, with the significant movement from institutional to community residential options for persons with mental retardation, one might anticipate an increase in the number of people with mental retardation becoming parents.

### 2. *Mental Retardation as a Factor in Termination Actions*    It is now firmly established that the mere status of mental retardation is not sufficient legal justification for permanently severing parental rights. There must be a specific showing that the condition of mental retardation results in the parent being unfit to provide adequate care for his or her child. Parental unfitness is the standard used in termination proceedings whether the parent has mental retardation or not. In the majority of states, the same statute for determining neglect is used for all parents. The approach in a minority of jurisdictions is to enact a separate statute for parents with mental retardation, although the standard mandated is essentially the same—parental unfitness (Retarded parents . . . , 1979).

The courts and many statutes also require an express consideration of the child's interests along with the parental unfitness criterion. The evidence must show, at minimum, that the parent's inability to care properly for the child causes or holds the potential for harm to the child if the child remains in the parent's custody, and that there is a probability that the parental unfitness will continue in the foreseeable future (Brakel et al. 1985).

The North Dakota statute is typical of many. The pertinent section follows:

> Termination is warranted where by reason of physical or mental incapacity the parent is unable to provide necessary parental care for the minor, and the court finds that the conditions and causes of the behavior, neglect, or incapacity are irremediable or will not be remedied by the parent, and that by reason thereof the minor is suffering or probably will suffer serious physical, mental, moral or emotional harm. . . . (N.D. Cent. Code § 14-15-19[3], 1981)

The extent to which mental retardation is a condition that is not completely understood, even by the experts in the field, means that a very careful balancing of interests between parent and child must take place.

> The requisite scientific knowledge about mental disability—its nature, duration, curability—as well as the sociological knowledge about what ultimately is best for parents or children which would give decision makers confidence in the substantive correctness of their decisions is wanting. As a result, perhaps, there has been a heavy emphasis on decision-making *procedure*—not merely to minimize the chance of error but to legitimize, as it were, decisions that are based on inadequate knowledge of what really is right or best. (Brakel . . . , 1985, p. 517)

Another statute, similar to North Dakota's, was upheld by a North Carolina court (*In re Montgomery*, 1984).[6] The court, in affirming the termination of parental rights based on long-term mental incapacity, found no violation of the due process or equal protection clauses of the Fourteenth Amendment. In so deciding, North Carolina followed the example of several other states.

One commentator recommends that the burden of proving that termination is in the best interests of the child should be placed squarely on the party seeking termination, in order to protect the constitutional rights of both parents and children. The factors to be considered in determining a child's best interests should be elucidated and should include consideration of the adoptability of the child. Further, the courts should clarify the extent to which termination hearings should be bifurcated, that is, divided into two phases (first, the adjudication of parental fitness and then the determination of the child's best interests) so that proper consideration can be given to the different issues at stake (Termination of . . . , 1985).

**3.  Administrative Agency Treatment of Parents with Mental Retardation**    The child welfare agency in each state plays a major role in the disposition of neglect cases. After the initial complaint is filed against a parent, an administrative agency employee, usually a social worker, makes a determination as to whether a full-scale investigation will occur. The author of a note on the treatment of parents with mental retardation in neglect proceedings believes that administrative agencies often intervene in cases where the parent(s) have mental retardation even when there has been no evidence of parental inadequacy (Retarded parents . . . , 1979).

After the investigative stage, the agency has the discretion to decide whether to dismiss the matter, attempt to correct the deficient caretaking through rehabilitative social services, or file a court action for neglect. One commentator has observed that agency personnel may believe that parents with mental retardation will eventually neglect their children (Retarded parents . . . , 1979) and that incompetence as an unavoidable feature of mental retardation cannot be remedied. (A case is cited

---

[6]The North Carolina statute included the provision that the "Court may terminate rights upon a finding. . .that the parent is incapable as a result of mental retardation, . . . .of providing for the proper care and supervision of the child. . .and there is reasonable probability that such incapacity will continue throughout the minority of the child." N.C. Gen. Stat. § 7A-289.32(7).

in which social services were denied to mentally retarded parents based on the belief that they could not benefit from services [Retarded parents . . . , 1979]). One case cited involved the termination of parental rights where there was no evidence of harm as the child was newborn (Retarded parents . . . , 1979).

When agencies assume that parents who have mental retardation will be inadequate parents, then the agency may proceed with an action where there is no evidence of deficient parenting. In other cases, agencies may proceed on the basis of evidence of inadequacy that would otherwise be treated as remediable if the parents did not have mental retardation. Subsequently, the court may simply ratify the administrative agencies' assumptions of inadequacy of parents with mental retardation (Retarded parents . . . , 1979).

**4.   *Rehabilitation Plans as a Means to Reunite Parents and Children***   The statutes in many states require that child welfare agencies and the courts use all reasonable and probable means to remedy a circumstance of deficient parenting before seeking a termination of the parent-child relationship (Retarded parents . . . , 1979). Similarly, constitutional principles require that the least restrictive or intrusive alternative to depriving an individual of a protected liberty interest be employed (Retarded parents . . . , 1979). Rehabilitative services for inadequate parents offer a less restrictive alternative than termination. For that reason a rehabilitation plan should be developed for a family whenever that is feasible. Application of the least restrictive principle should not be avoided simply because appropriate services are not readily available (Retarded parents . . . , 1979).

The case of *In re R.W.* (1986) applied a statute that allowed for termination of parental rights for failure to comply with a performance agreement, a technique used to identify and develop rehabilitative services intended to assist parents in improving their parenting capacity. The court held that the state must show abandonment, abuse, or neglect by clear and convincing evidence before parental rights can be permanently terminated and may not sever those rights solely on the basis of the parent's failure to substantially comply with the performance agreement with the state agency. The court stated its belief that allowing termination solely for failure to comply with a performance agreement vested too much discretion in the individual caseworkers.

In a law review comment on the case, the author criticizes the court's decision because it failed to address the extensive safeguards incorporated into state law. The author expresses the concern that the effect of the decision may be to allow children to "languish endlessly in foster care because there is no clear and convincing evidence of abuse, neglect or abandonment that would result in the severance of parental rights, yet reunification is untenable without costly supportive services which may be unavailable . . ." (Parental rights . . . , 1987, p. 298).

It seems, however, that the court's concern over the extent of caseworker discretion is legitimate in cases where the parent(s) have mental retardation. Excessive reliance upon the performance agreement and agency discretion could introduce an opportunity for value-laden and stereotyping judgments that could abridge fundamental parental rights. Judicial oversight should be exercised. The concern regarding "costly supportive services" is pertinent to cases involving parents with mental retardation. It is reasonable to expect that parents with mental retardation may require more intensive services for a longer period of time than would a person who does not have mental retardation. Denying rehabilitative services to those for whom it would be more costly than usual would deprive most parents with mental retardation of the least restrictive alternative to termination of parental rights.

   *5.* ***Adequacy of Parenting by Persons with Mental Retardation*** Other chapters in this volume deal directly with the issues of the types and levels of parenting skills observed in persons with mental retardation as well as techniques used to assist parents with mental retardation in the acquisition and maintenance of such skills. This section looks at measures of parent adequacy from the vantage point of the legal system.

> The legal system has generally emphasized three skills in neglect cases as essential for adequate parenting: love and affection, performing housekeeping tasks, and attending to the child's physical needs. . . .
>
> In cases involving retarded parents, some courts have added a fourth factor: stimulating the child intellectually. (Retarded parents . . . 1979, pp. 797–798)

Parents with mental retardation have the capacity to love and provide affection to their children. Courts have recognized that the parents were loving and affectionate toward their children even in cases that resulted in termination of parental rights (Retarded parents . . . , 1979). See, for example, *In re Jeannie Q.*, 1973 and *In re Orlando*, 1976.

The standard by which the legal system evaluates parental behavior focuses on the *adequacy* of care given to the child. An individual need not be the very best possible parent for the child nor provide the best possible and most intellectually stimulating home environment in order to measure up to the legal standard (*New Jersey Div. of Youth and Family Servs. v. B. W., 1977* [cited in Retarded Parents, 1979]). Statutory and constitutional principles prevent a state from terminating an individual's parental rights unless that person is proven to be incompetent at the requisite parenting skills. Mental retardation per se is not conclusive evidence that a parent is unable to provide his or her child with adequate care, affection, and education (Retarded parents . . . , 1979). An individual assessment of parenting skills should occur.

Courts and social service agencies should not base their decisions in neglect and termination cases upon the presumption that the class of parents with mental retardation is inadequate and neglectful unless this classification is supported in fact and is true of all parents in that class. A conclusive presumption that all parents who have mental retardation are inadequate is subject to constitutional challenge as a violation of the due process and equal protection clauses of the Fourteenth Amendment because it intrudes upon fundamental rights and is not necessarily or universally true (Retarded parents . . . , 1979).

## D. Recent Termination Cases
## Involving Parents with Mental Retardation

A review of recent reported cases involving parents with mental disabilities reveals that in the majority of instances the appellate courts upheld termination orders. There were a number of recurring issues addressed in termination proceedings during the 1980s. Those issues included: 1) procedural considerations; 2) the presence of extenuating circumstances in addition to the parent's mental retardation; 3) consideration of the nature, extent, and degree of success of support services provided; and 4) cases in which mental retardation in and of itself appeared to determine the outcome of the case. As might be expected, considerable variation is evident across state lines. Differences in statutes, regulations, resources available to social service agencies and the individuals they serve—all appear to influence decisions in this area of the law. Following is a review of the procedural considerations of representation, testimony, notice, and compulsory psychological examinations.

*1. Representation*   A frequently litigated issue is whether or not parents who have mental disabilities must be represented at termination hearings and by whom. The cases involving parents with mental disabilities should be considered in the context of the United States Supreme Court decision in *Lassiter v. Department of Social Services of Durham County* (1981). The *Lassiter* case involved an indigent mother incarcerated for second-degree murder whose parental rights were terminated. In finding for the State, the Court held that failure to provide the parent in these circumstances with legal counsel did not violate her due process rights. The condition of a mental disability could present a stronger case in support of requiring some type of legal representation.

A number of cases focused on the respective powers and responsibilities of guardians ad litem and legal counsel. In the case of *In re C.W.* (1987), the mother's attorney acted also as her guardian ad litem. Although the court stated that these appointments should be separated, it found that failure to do so did not result in prejudice to the mother in this instance. In its opinion, the court described the attorney's responsibility to be that of letting the client decide on his or her best wishes and then zealously representing those wishes. In contrast, the guardian ad litem's duty is to determine the ward's best interests without necessarily deferring to the ward's wishes.

The opposite result was reached in *South Carolina Department of Social Services v. McDow* (1981) in which the court held that the State cannot terminate parental rights of alleged incompetent parents without appointing a guardian ad litem even though the parents did have appointed legal counsel. The court, in its finding, emphasized the special trust relationship of the guardian ad litem to the parents, a relationship different from that of attorney to client.

Two other courts refused to find reversible error on the basis of failure to appoint both legal counsel and a guardian ad litem. In *Lisa M. v. California* (1986), the parent was represented by legal counsel only and in *In re JIW* (1985), the guardian ad litem, who also was an attorney, represented the mother. A conflicting result occurred in *In re Baby Girl Baxter* (1985). The court reversed the lower court's order of termination on the basis of denial of proper representation because the guardian ad litem also served as legal counsel for the mother, who had mental retardation.

*In re Guardianship of Alexander L.* (1985) was resolved by the court's order permitting the social service agency's attorney to attend the psychiatric examination of the mother on the same limited conditions as could the mother's attorney.

*2. Testimony* Generally, termination orders have withstood challenges of violations of psychologist-patient privilege. Courts have allowed psychologists to testify concerning parental fitness based upon their examinations of the parent, either because the court found no justifiable expectation of privilege, or for failure to object to the psychologist's testimony, or because the testimony was material and necessary to the court's determination. See *In re Adoption of Embick* (1986); *In re Welfare of Siegfried* (1985); *In re Elizabeth Q.* (1987); *In re Adoption of Abigail* (1986).

*3. Notice* A termination order was reversed and remanded in *In re Bryant* (1984) because the guardian-conservator of an incompetent institutionalized mother had not received notice of the termination proceedings.

*4. Compulsory Psychological Examinations* Courts have upheld orders compelling psychological examinations of parents against Fifth Amendment claims. *Michigan Department of Social Services v. Beam* (1985); *Catholic Child Care Society of Diocese of Brooklyn v. Evelyn F.* (1985); *In re C.J.H.* (1985).

*5. Limitations Resulting from Mental Retardation as a Basis for Termination* A termination order was upheld based on psychological evaluations of the biological mother and grandmother, who respectively had mental retardation and borderline intelligence, indicating that the child was likely to suffer emotional or mental neglect and injury if placed with either of them. *Warren v. Florida Department of Health and Rehabilitative Services* (1987).

A Colorado court set aside a voluntary relinquishment by two parents with mental retardation because the parents proved that they did not understand the significance and consequences of their act of giving up their rights to their child. It was noted that the child had not yet been placed for adoption. See *In re J.B.P.* (1980).

A termination order was affirmed in a case where the father, who might have been capable of acquiring essential parenting skills, relied instead upon the mother who had mental retardation to take care of the children. The court concluded that the mother lacked the mental ability to provide proper care. See *In re G.C.P.* (1984). In its opinion, the court seemed to rely primarily upon the mother's status of having mental retardation. According to the court, "(t)here was no indication of intentional abuse," and the finding of neglect was supported by only nominal reference to substandard housekeeping. The decision was based in part on the psychologist's testimony that "because of their mental deficiencies," the mother and father could "not overcome their parenting deficiencies." No mention was made of a formal rehabilitation plan, although there was some indication of agency intervention.

**6. Other Extenuating Circumstances in Addition to Mentally Retarded Status**    Frequently the cases report situations beyond the fact of the parent's mental retardation that influence the court's determination. The parent(s) may have other indicators of potential inadequacy in caring for their children. In some cases, termination orders were upheld where the parent was unable to provide proper care for the child due to symptoms and/or diagnoses of mental retardation and mental illness. See *In re Lori Jean S.* (1985); *In re Campbell* (1983) (child was removed as a newborn); *In re Beyers* (1986); *In re Welfare of T.M.D.* (1987); *Williams v. Alabama Department of Pensions and Security* (1984); *Sexton v. J.E.H.* (1984). Beyond the complications of an additional disabling condition in the above cited cases, there was also evidence in some of the cases that the children themselves either had special needs, had already suffered some deprivation or injury, or that older children in the family had so suffered.

In circumstances where the parent's only disability was mental retardation, the added factor of detrimental effect on the child, either in the past or as a future potential, was sufficient to uphold a termination decision. See *E.L.B. v. Texas Department of Human Services* (1987); *In re Brown* (1987).

Another extenuating circumstance encountered by the courts is that the child himself or herself is disabled or otherwise presents special needs. This additional feature is sometimes a further complication to situations discussed above (e.g., parental dual diagnosis). A Massachusetts court affirmed termination of parental rights in *In re Adoption of Abigail* (1986) based on the mother's mental retardation and the child's neurological and psychological disorders. The court concluded that "if the question were simply one of the mother's limited intelligence, matched with a child of normal needs, there might not be a lawful basis for the radical step of terminating the link between the natural mother and child." This child's special needs, however, were relevant because they affected whether "*this* particular mother . . . can be a fit parent to *this* particular child." A similar holding was reached in *In re Welfare of B.L.W.* (1986) in which the child had fetal dilantin syndrome caused by the mother's overdose of antiseizure medication during pregnancy and also in *In re K.M.T.* (1986) in which the daughter had mild mental retardation and attention limitation disorder. See also *In re David E.* (1985) and the *Williams* and *Sexton* cases cited above.

The United States Supreme Court refused to review a finding of child abuse and neglect against parents who had mental retardation in the case of *Ensign v. Illinois.* The child had microcephaly and was injured at an early age when accidentally dropped on a hard surface.

**7.  Nature and Extent of Support Services** There is, of course, considerable variation from state to state with respect to statutory demands, administrative standards and regulations, and available resources in the area of support services provided to parents with mental retardation. Additionally, the legal system is variable in its interpretation and application of state laws.

In some cases, courts affirmed termination orders either because the parents failed to show an active interest in their children or failed to cooperate with the social service agencies' attempts at rehabilitative services. See *In re Welfare of P.J.K.* (1985) and *In re Alfredo HH* (1985). However, the court dismissed the termination petition in *In re Shaneek Christal W.* (1986) for failure to meet the clear and convincing evidence standard because the petitioner failed to rule out the possibility that if the mother had cooperated with treatment, she could have been rehabilitated.

Courts have reversed termination orders in cases where the social service agency failed to provide rehabilitative services at all. The appellate court in *In re R.S.* (1985) ruled that the lower court had not adequately explored less detrimental alternatives to termination of parental rights of a mother who had mild mental retardation.

A few courts have gone further and provided guidance regarding measures of adequacy and quality of rehabilitative services. At the court of appeals level in *In re P.J.K.* (1984), consideration was given to the fact that special parenting classes and counseling were not available for parents with mental retardation. The lack of those specialized services was one factor in finding the rehabilitation plan inadequate. The Minnesota Supreme Court, however, reversed the appellate court and upheld the termination order. In looking at the issue of rehabilitative services aimed at increasing parenting skills, the Supreme Court focused on the father's inability to benefit from the group parenting classes that had been provided rather than on the possible inappropriateness of those services. See *In re P.J.K.* (1985).

Similarly, indicators of the quality and quantity of support services necessary to support a termination finding were given in the case of *In re Petition of Catholic Guardian Society* (1986). The mother, who had mild mental retardation, had difficulty making daily basic caretaking decisions and could not provide adequate structure or supervision for her four children. She did, however, have some minimal coping skills and a significant emotional attachment to her children. She had already been provided assistance in managing her money, obtaining housing, and visiting her children while they were in custody of social services. The court based its reversal of the termination order on failure of the evidence to establish the mother's inability to care for her children in the foreseeable future. No history of maladaptive parenting was shown while the children were in their mother's care nor had the mother been provided with any psychiatric or psychological services. Diligent efforts had not been made to strengthen or encourage the parent-child relationship. The court noted that "in the 'post-Willowbrook' era, social services agencies need to be more sensitive to the specialized needs of mentally retarded parents whose children come into their care."

Nevertheless, in a number of cases, courts did affirm termination orders on the basis of evidence showing that rehabilitation efforts had been unsuccessful. An individualized reunification plan was developed and eventually discontinued because the mother failed to make sufficient progress in *In re Lori D.* (1986). The court in *In re L.A.V.* (1987) found that the State had made all reasonable efforts after developing several service plan contracts and establishing goals to learn child care and basic housekeeping. Despite the long history of receiving state agency assistance, both parents lacked parenting skills and showed a minimal ability to achieve the identified goals or to retain any instruction on child rearing.

In a case involving a mother who did not have mental retardation but who had a personality disorder, the court upheld a termination decision because the experts agreed that the mother needed 1–5 years of intensive therapy and the results were unpredictable. See *In re Joseph P.* (1987). This case raises concerns with regard to parents who have mental retardation and may be likely to require intensive support services for a significant period of time. Another instance in which the court upheld a termination order because the rehabilitation plan failed involved a parent with a mental disability. In *In re L.G.* (1987), the court stated that a rehabilitation plan was not rendered inappropriate just because it did not work.

The case of *In re S.W.* (1986) included compounded issues of mental retardation, emotional disturbance, lack of cooperation with social workers, and evidence of neglect. The court relied upon the extensive history of intervention by social service agencies including protective payee, homemaker, nutrition aide, parent counseling, transportation, and referral services to support its decision that, in this circumstance, termination was the least restrictive alternative available.

The court in *West Virginia v. C.N.S.* (1984) affirmed a termination order based on the failure of support services for parents who had mental retardation and exhibited difficulty in showing affection toward their children.

An interesting Massachusetts case suggests an alternative that should have been considered. The appeals court vacated and remanded a termination order despite the facts that the mother had mental retardation, an alcohol problem, and an alcoholic husband; the oldest child had a psychiatric disorder; the youngest of the four children had a speech impairment; and there was evidence that the children had formed emotional ties to their foster parents. The court found that the mother's past unfitness did not constitute clear and convincing evidence of her current unfitness. Furthermore, the lower court erred by considering the children's best interests only collectively and not individually as well. The mother's fitness should have been determined by considering the return of any one or more of the children, not only the possibility of returning all the children. See *Petitions of Department of Social Services to Dispense with Consent to Adoption* (1985).

## VIII.   RECOMMENDATIONS AND CONCLUSIONS

When child welfare agencies and ultimately the legal system intervene because there is actual or potential harm to a child, the same factors should be considered in cases involving parents with mental retardation as are considered when the parents do not have mental retardation. Evidence of harm to the child and proof of deficiencies in child-rearing abilities are the relevant factors. Evidence of IQ scores should not be determinative. An analogy can be drawn to the field of employment discrimination. Just as employment practices must meet the requirement of job-relatedness so should the standards applied in neglect cases be based upon an assessment of parenting skills. Administrative agencies and courts should be evaluating the skills and attributes necessary to provide adequate care for children, not solely or even at all the intelligence quotient of the parent. Skills should be written in behavioral terms so that they can be identified and evaluated with a fair degree of objectivity.

If the court, after consideration of evidence appropriate and relevant to the issue of child-rearing skills and abilities does find evidence of deficiencies, then the principle of least restrictive alternative should be applied. At that stage, rehabilitative services should be ordered whenever they present a feasible alternative to removing the child from the natural home. Only in determining the nature and degree of social services that are to be provided to a family should the mental retardation of the parent be considered. The administrative convenience or cost of providing the indicated services should not be allowed as an excuse for failing to provide them. The fundamental rights to retain custody, to rear one's own child, and to preserve the family unit should not be abridged for lack of availability of appropriate services.

The child welfare system's and legal system's treatment of parents with mental retardation should not only conform to constitutional standards, but should also reflect current knowledge and state-of-the-art practices. Parents who have mental retardation should be afforded a reasonable opportunity to acquire and maintain the parenting skills necessary to enable them to provide adequate care for their children. With the advent of the supported employment concept, new horizons have opened up for persons with mental retardation. Not long before this concept, even some experts in the field of disabilities would have expressed skepticism at the notion that persons with severe disabilities could be employed in the real work world for real pay. Opportunities for acquiring parenting skills should not be limited by false barriers or unwarranted low expectations. The same creativity and dedication of re-sources should be made toward the goal of family integrity as has been made in the employment area. These reforms should be adopted to ensure that the legal system accords parents with mental retardation the same rights to raise children and enjoy family life that society permits all other parents.

## REFERENCES

Adoption Assistance and Child Welfare Act. (1980). 42 U.S.C. § 627–628 (Supp. V 1981) and 42 U.S.C. § 671–676 (Supp. V 1981).

Areen, J. (1975). Intervention between parent and child, a reappraisal of the state's role in child neglect and abuse cases. *Georgetown Law Journal, 63*, 887.

Brakel, S., Parry, F., & Weiner, B. (1985). *The mentally disabled and the law* (3rd ed.) (pp. 516, 517, 520, 544–546). Chicago: American Bar Foundation.

Catholic Child Care Society of Diocese of Brooklyn v. Evelyn F., 492 N.Y.S. 2d 338 (N.Y. Fam. Ct. 1985).

Comment: Parental rights in emotional abuse and neglect cases—In re Interest of Hochstetler. (1985). *Creighton Law Review, 18*, 449–451.

Comment: Termination of parental rights. (1986). *Wake Forest Law Review, 21*, 431–432.

E.L.B. v. Texas Department of Human Services, 732 S.W.2d 785 (Tex. Ct. App. 1987).

Ensign v. Illinois, 147 Ill. App. 3d 1164, 111 Ill. Dec. 236, 512 N.E. 2d 140, No. 87-135, cert. denied 11/30/87, 56 U.S.L.W. 3383.

Garrison, M. (1983). Why terminate parental rights? *Stanford Law Review, 35*, 423–426.

Ginsberg v. New York, 390 U.S. 629 (1968).

Goldstein, J., Freud, A., & Solnit, A. (1973). *Beyond best interests of the child*. New York: Free Press.

Hayes, S., & Morse, M. (1983). Adoption and termination proceedings in Wisconsin: Straining the wisdom of Solomon. *Marquette Law Review, 66*, 443, 444.

Hershkowitz, S. (1985). Due process and the termination of parental rights. *Family Law Quarterly, 19*, 245–258.

In re Adoption of Abigail, 499 N.E.2d 1234 (Mass. Ct. App. 1986).

In re Adoption of Embick, 506 A.2d 455 (Pa. Super. Ct. 1986).

In re Alfredo HH, 486 N.Y.S.2d 689 (N.Y. App. Div. 1985).

In re Baby Girl Baxter, 479 N.E.2d 257 (Ohio Sup. Ct. 1985).

In re Beyers, 496 N.E.2d 1248 (Ill. App. Ct. 1986).

In re Brown, 736 P.2d 1355 (Idaho Ct. App. 1987).

In re Bryant, 689 P.2d 1203 (Kan. Ct. App. 1984).

In re Campbell, 468 N.E.2d 93 (Ohio Ct. App. 1983).

In re C.J.H., 371 N.W.2d 345 (S.D. Sup. Ct. 1985).

In re C.L.M., 625 S.W.2d 613 (Mo. 1981).

In re C.W., 414 N.W.2d 277 (Neb. Sup. Ct. 1987).

In re David E., 496 A.2d 229 (Conn. Ct. App. 1985).

In re Elizabeth Q., 511 N.Y.S.2d 181 (N.Y. App. Div. 1987).

In re G.C.P., 680 S.W.2d 429 (Mo. Ct. App. 1984).

In re Guardianship of Alexander L., 493 N.Y.S.2d 157 (N.Y. App. Div. 1985).

In re J.B.P., 608 P.2d 847 (Colo. Ct. App. 1980).

In re Jeannie Q., 32 Cal. App.3d 288, 294, 299, 107 Cal. Rptr. 646, 651, 654 (2d Dist. 1973).

In re J.I.W., 695 S.W.2d 513 (Mo. Ct. App. 1985).

In re Joseph P., 532 A.2d 1013 (Me. Sup. Jud. Ct. 1987).

In re K.M.T., 390 N.W.2d 371 (Minn. Ct. App. 1986).

In re L.A.V., 516 So.2d 1315 (La. Ct. App. 1987).

In re L.G., 737 P.2d 431 (Colo. Ct. App. 1987).

In re Lori D., 510 A.2d 421 (R.I. Sup. Ct. 1986).

In re Lori Jean S., 494 N.Y.S.2d 373 (N.Y. App. Div. 1985).

In re Montgomery, 311 N.C. 101, 316, S.E.2d 246 (1984).

In re Orlando F., 40 N.Y.2d 103, 110, 351 N.E.2d 711, 715, 386 N.Y.S.2d 64, 67 (1976).

In re Petition of Catholic Guardian Society, 499 N.Y.S.2d 587 (N.Y. Fam. C., Kings Cty. 1986).

In re P.J.K., 356 N.W.2d 69 (Minn. Ct. App. 1984).

In re P.J.K., 369 N.W.2d 286 (Minn. 1985).

In re R.S., 213 Cal. Rptr. 690 (Cal. Ct. App. 1985).

In re R.W., 495 So.2d 133 (Fla. 1986).

In re Shaneek Christal W., 504 N.Y.S.2d 748 (N.Y. App. Div. 1986).

In re S.W., 398 N.W.2d 136 (S.D. Supp. Ct. 1986).

In re Welfare of B.L.W., 395 N.W.2d 426 (Minn. Ct. App. 1986).

In re Welfare of P.J.K., 369 N.W.2d 286 (Minn. Sup. Ct. 1985).

In re Welfare of Siegfried, 708 P.2d 402 (Wash. Ct. App. 1985).

In re Welfare of T.M.D., 410 N.W.2d 72 (Minn. Ct. App. 1987).

Lassiter v. Department of Social Services of Durham County, 452 U.S. 18 (1981).

Lisa M. v. California, 225 Cal. Rptr. 7 (Cal. Ct. App. 1986).

Meyer v. Nebraska, 262 U.S. 390 (1923).

Michigan Department of Social Services v. Beam, 371 N.W.2d 446 (Mich. Ct. App. 1985).

Minnesota adopts a best interests standard in parental rights termination proceedings: In re J.J.B. (1987). *Minnesota Law Review, 71,* 1263–1292.

Moore v. City of Cleveland, 431 U.S. 494 (1977).

N.D. Cent. Code § 14-15-19(3) (1981).

New Jersey Division of Youth & Family Services v. B.W., 384 A.2d 923, 926 (1977).

Parental rights termination: Are the interests of parents, children, and the state mutually exclusive? (1987). *Stetson Law Review, 17,* 295–299, 300, 302, 304.

Parham v. J.R., 442 U.S. 584, 602 (1979).

Price v. Price, 255 S.E.2d 652 (N.C. Ct. App. 1979).

Petitions of Department of Social Services to Dispense with Consent to Adoption, 482 N.E.2d 5335 (Mass. App. Ct. 1985).

Quilloin v. Walcott, 434 U.S. 246 (1978).

Retarded parents in neglect proceedings: The erroneous assumption of parental inadequacy. (1979). *Stanford Law Review, 31,* 785–788, 790–795, 797, 798, 801.

Santosky v. Kramer, 455 U.S. 745, 747, 748, 753, 765, 769 (1982).

Sexton v. J.E.H., 355 N.W.2d 828 (N.D. Sup. Ct. 1984).

Smith v. Organization of Foster Families 431 U.S. 816 (1977).

South Carolina Department of Social Services v. McDow, 280 S.E.2d 208 (1981).

Stanley v. Illinois, 405 U.S. 645, 651 (1972).

Termination of parental rights: Putting love in its place. (1985). *North Carolina Law Review, 63,* 1177–1183, 1187, 1188.

Termination of parental rights—Suggested reforms and responses. (1977–1978). *Journal of Family Law, 16,* 239–244.

Wakefield, W. (1983). Annotation validity of state statute providing for termination of parental rights. *American Law Reports, 22*(4), 778–779.

Wald, M. (1975). State intervention on behalf of "neglected" children, a search for realistic students. *Stanford Law Review, 27,* 985.

Wald, M. (1976). State intervention on behalf of neglected children: Standards for removal of children from their homes, monitoring the status of children in foster care and termination of parental rights. *Stanford Law Review, 28,* 623.

Warren v. Florida Department of Health and Rehabilitative Services, 501 So.2d 706 (Fla. Dist. Ct. App. 1987).

West Virginia v. C.N.S., 319 S.E.2d 775 (W.Va. Sup. Ct. 1984).

Williams v. Alabama Department of Pensions and Security, 460 So.2d 1348 (Ala. Div. App. 1984).

# 11 | Parents with Mental Retardation and Developmental Disabilities

## Ethical issues in parenting

Dennis A. Brodeur

**C**hildren need direction and assistance to mature physically, emotionally, spiritually, educationally, and socially. What happens when parents cannot provide this direction? Are parents who have mental retardation different from other inadequate parents who are not labeled as having mental disabilities, but are equally unable, or less able, to raise their own children? Can society create policies that affect all parents who have mental retardation without individual consideration of circumstances, place, and time? What are the rights of children, and how should children's rights be understood? Are there parameters to guide discussion in this area?

There is not a great deal of ethics literature on this subject. More attention is focused on the legal rights of mentally retarded adults for marriage and for appropriate sexual relationships within marriage, including for procreation. But the procreative concerns are secondary to the sexual needs and desires of adults with mental retardation and do not address their parenting abilities. There is little discussion about the rights of children or their needs for an acceptable level of care for growth into independent adulthood.

The focus of Chapter 11 is the ethical issues that emerge when one examines the ability of parents with mental retardation or developmental disabilities to care for their own children. This discussion will attempt to identify some ethical principles that apply to all persons and then explore their meaning for parents with mental retardation. It will also attempt to establish 12 ethical principles to guide current decisions and to further this discussion in society.


## ETHICAL CONSIDERATIONS

Ethical concerns focus on the person. Each individual is sacred, meaning that he or she must not be used as a means to an end, be treated unjustly, be discriminated against, or have his or her dignity violated by other individuals or by society. Each individual's integrity must be respected. A person's cognitive status does not change this. A person's abilities and potential may be different because of mental retardation. But this does not justify automatic classification of a person into one group or excluding a person from specific activities or behaviors.

The *rights* of persons that flow from the recognition of the dignity and sacredness of each person belong to persons with mental retardation as much as to any other person in society. The rights to socialize, to be educated, to receive medical care, to marry, and to pursue a meaningful job must all be respected.

*Justice* for all is a basic expression of the ethical way individuals should treat one another. Justice requires that individuals be treated equitably. Equitable treatment does not mean that each person is treated in exactly the same way but that the circumstances particular to each individual are considered carefully before policies, decisions, or activities are undertaken that may result in discrimination. It is unjust to discriminate against persons with mental retardation solely on the basis of cognitive limitation (Friedman, 1976).

These concerns also suggest that society periodically reexamine its assumptions and attitudes toward individuals with mental retardation to ensure that the assumptions and attitudes are not erroneous or self-fulfilling prophecies. If this is not done, unjust structures and unjust actions will result. Examples of this occurring in contemporary society are not hard to find. For example, persons with mental retardation are over-represented in prison populations at three times the rate that they exist in society at large. One might conclude that this indicates that individuals with mental retardation are more likely to have criminal tendencies or to act out criminal tendencies. Or it can mean that when individuals with mental retardation are caught in suspicious settings or are accused of committing a crime, their civil rights are more likely to be violated than those of other members of society, or their ability to secure an effective defense is more limited.

The eugenics movement in the United States in the early 1900s is another example of how false assumptions and attitudes result in unjust structures or acts. It was believed that adults with mental retardation would give birth to a disproportionate number of children with mental retardation. Mental retardation was perceived to be a hereditary trait passed on through the genetic makeup of the man and woman. Mandatory sterilization, especially for women, would thus reduce the number of people born with mental retardation and would improve the quality-of-life for society as a whole. However, a more careful examination of the data ultimately gave rise to a different view of these attitudes and assumptions. The eugenics movement involving mandatory sterilization for all citizens with mental retardation is today considered to represent a violation of basic human rights and, therefore, to be unethical.

Expressions of justice are made concrete in human socialization. Persons with mental retardation, like all other individuals, are social by nature, not by choice. It is only through a social environment that any person learns to interact, speak, and think, to realize whatever potential or capability he or she has. Fostering a positive social environment is a moral commitment that a society makes to its citizens. This is more imperative for those who are vulnerable or who are more likely to be discriminated against.

Developing an appropriate social environment for individuals with mental retardation means creating an environment where the least restraints are present. Environments of least restraint do not maximize freedom in an unbridled sense but are designed to help individuals achieve their fullest possible potential. When environments must become more restrictive, this needs to happen in order to protect the physical or emotional well-being of the person or to protect the person from doing avoidable harm to others. The need for restraints of any type does not justify unethical practices.

The social dimension of human life also requires that society meet the life-care needs of those who are vulnerable. Again, those who are vulnerable include persons with mental retardation. They cannot be abandoned or hidden but must receive humanized care. Humanized care is the operative principle that checks a too rigid restrictive environment, especially in those rare circumstances where institutionalization seems to be the appropriate alternative for individuals with mental retardation. Humanized care, in family life, can call forth the creativity necessary to develop new structures that support family-based programs for adults with mental retardation.

Marriage is an opportunity for individuals to express love, affection, and give care, and to build a partnership of life and love. It is an element of the social existence of human beings in society. Many persons with mental retardation are able to express love and affection and to pursue healthy interdependent relationships. The right to marriage, however, does not necessarily include a right to parenting. For example, in circumstances where infertility problems or sterility prevents a couple from having a child, a further demand for a child cannot be placed upon society. It is hard to prove that individuals, even in the context of marriage, have a right to have children. When it comes to children in the family setting of a couple with mental retardation, the rights and needs of the children will have to be carefully balanced against the rights and needs of the parents.

There is a strong legal and ethical presumption in favor of biological parents being able to care for their children. This presumption should probably not be changed. Adults with mental retardation should be accorded the same presumption. In the case of persons with mental retardation, however, there are some indications that, even in the best of circumstances, parents will not be able to meet the child's long-range adolescent needs. To date, few creative structures exist to help parents with mental retardation raise children during this difficult period. It is difficulties such as these that give rise to practical problems when making decisions about the parenting abilities of adults with mental retardation.

This issue becomes more critical when one recognizes the significance that society has always placed upon the family unit as the cornerstone of all other social activities. As such, the family unit needs to be protected, promoted, and developed and should be broken apart only in cases where there is ample evidence that family life is more destructive than helpful. However, the very importance of family life in social structures indicates the seriousness with which these issues about individuals with mental retardation and developmental disabilities as parents should be addressed. Is it possible to neglect some members of the human family, namely the children of adults with mental retardation, in order to protect the rights of mentally retarded adults themselves? What bridges can be developed to provide excellent care and opportunity for children in these settings, while at the same time being sensitive and respectful to the needs and rights of the mentally retarded parents?

Society has a moral obligation to protect those who are vulnerable—young, weak, sick, frail, or very old. Vulnerable people can too easily be lost in the shuffle in society, be discriminated against, lose their rights, or not be accorded the same dignity of other less vulnerable persons. Society supports vulnerable people through special programs such as special education, guardianship programs, and other supportive and creative environments that help to meet the physical, psychological, emotional, spiritual, and social dimensions of the human being. It would be easy to resolve all ethical dilemmas of discrimination or injustice if all discrimination and injustice took place only between those who are most vulnerable and those who are considered to be the strongest members of society. However, the occurrence of children being raised by parents who have mental retardation raises questions about two groups of vulnerable people. Balancing these concerns is difficult.

Children are a significant group of vulnerable people in society. Protecting children and helping children to grow and realize their full potential consumes considerable resources in society. Guaranteed public education through 12 years of schooling, protective custody services, guardianship, a juvenile court system, and a different set of rules and principles by which we judge the behavior of minor citizens are all indicative of the importance that society places on caring for them. This very commitment has a bearing on issues about balancing the rights of children with the rights and interests of their parents.

Problems arise because adults with mental retardation want to be parents. This may be an acceptable desire, and they may be able to realize the challenge of parenting when children are younger. But things can change when children are older. As children become adolescents, the strengths, skills, and intellectual capacities of the parents may create a series of critical problems that can hurt the family unit, prevent the child from realizing his or her potential, and frustrate the mentally retarded adults' desire to be good parents.

Another difficulty is whether society should wait for the family to become dysfunctional before stepping in or has an obligation to step in prior to the onset of family dysfunction. In almost all circumstances a judge or social worker will wait until there is clear and ample evidence of family dysfunction before removing a child from the home for either a short period of time or permanently (Goldstein, Freud, & Solnit, 1973). In the case of parents with mental retardation, how does one balance a situation in which family dysfunction is evident against other kinds of difficult circumstances where the problems are not as readily apparent? How does one work with the long-term effects of a child separated from his or her biological family when he or she is older? If such separation becomes necessary, is there more psychological and emotional damage done to the child in the long run? What does protecting vulnerable children mean in light of these questions?

## ETHICAL GUIDELINES

In view of the above concerns, the following ethical principles are offered as a guide to the decision-making process when questions arise about parents with mental retardation maintaining custody and care of their children. These principles articulate some of the values mentioned above and can help decision-makers think through the issues involved in fostering or terminating parental rights.

### 1.   Family Units Are to Be Upheld, Promoted, and Developed

A sound social fabric is necessary for anyone to live and flourish in society. Family units remain the centerpiece of social living. There are many issues that erode public support for family units in contemporary society. The situation is more complicated when adults with mental retardation are expected to provide for the development and growth of their children so that their children can become mature, functional, and loving adults. New and creative structures might need to be developed to help some persons with mental retardation with their parenting so that children in these family units will receive the necessary guidance and direction to realize their potential. It is necessary to develop decision-making processes that both respect a family unit's rights and promote a child's development.

## 2.  Children Are Not Chattel and
## Their Rights Need to Be Developed and Respected

Any notion that children are the property of their parents and that children cannot be taken away from their parents because parents have a first claim on them should be seriously questioned. Children are not property; they are persons who, with some luck and development, will grow to be adults. Little work has been done to identify a set of children's rights that would help guarantee that children have opportunities to grow into normal adulthood. A variety of other questions have to be raised, especially in the case of children of parents who have mental retardation. Developing rights of such children points to the fact that there are many areas in society where parenting skills and parenting abilities need to be better addressed.

## 3.  Children's Problems Are Not Confined to
## Those of Children of Parents with Mental Retardation

Before one takes children away from parents with mental retardation, one has to recognize that there are many pressures in society that mitigate against children receiving a solid upbringing. Society cannot step into all cases of dysfunctional parents or family settings. One must also presume that parents love, care for, and cherish their children and want only the best for them. Only when it becomes clear that this cannot be done should children be taken away from their parents. In the case of parents with mental retardation, however, it is frequently clear that parents who do love, care for, and have affection for their children need tremendous help to guide their children through later childhood and adolescent years. Some parents with mental retardation may be up to the challenge, others may not. Parents who have mental retardation should not be classified as unfit parents de facto but must be judged like any other parents who are experiencing difficulties raising their children appropriately.

## 4. Mental Retardation and
## Other Mental Disabilities in Children
## Do Not Necessarily Result from Being Born of or Raised by
## Parents Who Have Mental Retardation or Other Mental Disabilities

According to the eugenics movement in the early twentieth century, persons with mental retardation would conceive and bring into the world only mentally retarded children. Today, we know this is often not the case. Removing children from families or preventing individuals with mental retardation from having children on the assumption that they will have children with mental retardation is an unethical assumption based on incorrect facts.

## 5. Difficulties with Parenting
## Must Be Faced and May Require Societal Intervention

It was noted above that parents with mental retardation are but one group of parents who may have difficulty raising their children. But their problems, like the parenting problems of many other families, need to be addressed in a forthright manner. Agonizing over how to protect the rights of the children so as not to violate anyone's rights is an important and necessary responsibility of society. But ethical activity does not end by analyzing a problem or agonizing over its difficulties. Ultimately, decisions have to be made and action must be taken. This must be done within the context of a given society. Social norms should be established to address not only short-term, but also long-term effects of parental capabilities.

## 6. Criteria for Successful Parenting Need To Be Developed

Courts, social service agencies, and health care providers frequently make determinations about the fitness of parents to raise their children. Sometimes these determinations are correct and sometimes they are not. Sometimes determinations can lead to the breakup of a family unit. These judgments can create more difficulties when children are taken away from the biological parents with whom they have formed strong ties and are placed in different environments, hopefully to be nurtured and developed in a more appropriate setting. Frequently, when children are taken away from their parents, even if these parents have been tremendously abusive, psychological problems such as guilt, anxiety, and a strong bonding or attachment to the physically abusive parent can occur. Significant time, medical treatment, and psychotherapy may be necessary for these children to gain an adequate sense of self and to be able to enter into meaningful relationships with others. Criteria that are developed and used in society probably need to be honed more carefully so that the judgments of judges, social workers, and others are not arbitrary. These criteria can also help society determine when it will be necessary to remove children from families with parents who have mental retardation. These are hard decisions, but for the well-being of the child these decisions are probably best made during pregnancy or immediately after birth, even if the parents are capable of caring for the child for the first few years of life.

## 7.  Extenuating Circumstances for the Child, the Family, and the Parents Must Be Addressed

Extenuating circumstances often color both the specific problems encountered in an individual situation and the six principles listed above. For parents with mental retardation, different support group structures may allow them the ability to keep their children in the home and to provide adequate opportunity for their children's education, development, and well-being. A variety of group homes, extended family networks, and other support structures may provide what cannot be given by the mentally retarded parents by themselves. If appropriate support structures can be developed and reasonably guaranteed for the future of the child's dependency, decisions to leave children with their mentally retarded parents might be more justifiable. In terms of extenuating circumstances for families, there is little doubt that adults with mental retardation can often provide the affection and love that are a significant part of any child's development and growth. But other issues must also be addressed. These issues include the child's educational development, emotional maturity, social interaction, and other areas of concern that parents with mental retardation may not be able to provide.

In addition there can be many extenuating circumstances for the child. What is the child's own mental ability? What are the child's physical or health care needs? What are the child's personal needs? If the child has special needs, the parent with mental retardation, even in a strong group support structure, may not be able to provide adequately for the child.

## 8.  Children Sometimes Require
## Hard Decisions To Be Made for Them

Good will and the best of intentions are very important parts of social life, but they are not always translated into action. Sometimes when good intentions are not realized, harm is done. A child especially may want family life to work but cannot carry that burden of making it so. A hard decision will have to be made for the child. This decision must be made if society wants to value the protection it provides for those who are vulnerable.

## 9.  Children's Long-Term Needs Cannot
## Be Sacrificed for Short-Term Adult Gains

Children's long-term needs balanced against short-term adult gains are critical in the discussion of leaving children in the home with parents who have mental retardation or placing the child into a different setting. At stake, frequently, for the child, are a number of long-term issues, specifically, the child's ability to mature, develop, be educated, and function in society as an independent adult. It is exactly these long-term goals for the child that might be compromised by leaving the child with his or her biological parents. In order to ensure that the long-term interests of the child are not sacrificed to the short-term gains of the adults, the child needs mentioned above have to be addressed.

## 10.  One Must Distinguish the
## Marital Rights of Persons with Mental Retardation
## from the Parental Rights of Persons with Mental Retardation

It is true that persons with mental retardation have the same need for affection, love, care, and sexual expression as do other individuals. To deny their right to meet these needs is unethical (De la Cruz & LaVeck, 1973). One cannot confuse the right to a partner and love with a right to a child. While in many circumstances adults who have mental retardation will conceive and bear children, this does not give rise to an automatic right to raise that child. This, of course, raises serious questions about birth control for persons with mental retardation.

## 11.  Sterilization of the Man or Woman, Permanently
## or Temporarily, Must Be Addressed in a Forthright Manner

The issue of sterilization involves education, perhaps some supervision, and a respect for the religious and ethical traditions of the individual involved. Mandatory sterilization is not a solution to the parenting dilemma of adults with mental retardation. Involuntary sterilization of either a man or a woman is a fundamental violation of a person's body and sexuality, a violation of a person's body and sexuality, a violation of a person's life. In fact, mandatory sterilization, previous to marriage, for all adults with mental retardation is a discriminatory action that society cannot permit. In addition, mandatory sterilization before marriage will not resolve the problems of mentally retarded individuals conceiving and bearing children outside of marriage. To require mandatory sterilization of all individuals previous to the onset of puberty is utterly unjust (National Institute on Mental Retardation, 1980).

## 12. Mentally Retarded Adults Must Have Their Rights Protected in the Area of Marriage, Sexuality, and Family Life

In the decision to terminate parental rights for adults with mental retardation, a delicate balancing of their rights to life, love, and a family with the basic and fundamental needs of the child is required. Because most children born to adults with mental retardation will not be mentally retarded, society has to balance a child's need for a different environment in which to have successful life experiences against an innate human desire on the part of the mentally retarded parents to have and maintain their own family. As noted above, it may be possible to develop some creative structures that will allow parents with mental retardation to maintain their families. But many extended families may not want to live together or commit themselves to geographical proximity to ensure that the children of persons with mental retardation have opportunities to develop and grow as they should.

## CONCLUSION

The 12 ethical guidelines outlined above need to be fleshed out more than they are in this short chapter. Additional reflection on how the principles can be worked into actual societal commitments is crucial. The fundamental question is whether the individual rights of a person or a couple override the social commitment of life and fundamental societal nature of life. In part, this chapter argues that societal structures and societal commitment are primary concerns in ethical issues and sometimes supersede individual rights. In society, however, abrogating individual rights for societal concerns is almost never done. Nonetheless, with parents who have mental retardation certain behavior patterns may be more evident and more predictable than in other equally or more disadvantaged settings in which the parents do not have mental retardation. This reality cannot be ignored. One can question whether parents with mental retardation are being held to a different standard than other parents, and the answer may be yes. But perhaps the question should be asked whether other parents should be held to the same standard that parents with mental retardation are expected to meet. And perhaps the real question is—how much does society value its children?

## REFERENCES

De la Cruz, F.F., & LaVeck, G.D. (Eds.). (1973). *Human sexuality and the mentally retarded.* New York: Brunner/Mazel.

Friedman, P.R. (1976). *The rights of mentally retarded persons: The Basic ACLU Guide for the Mentally Retarded Person's Rights.* New York: Avon Books.

Goldstein, J., Freud, A., & Solnit, A.J. (1973). *Beyond the best interests of the child.* New York: Free Press.

National Institute on Mental Retardation. (1980). *Sterilization and mental handicap.* Downsview, Ontario: National Institute on Mental Retardation.

# Conclusion

Barbara Y. Whitman
Pasquale J. Accardo

**M**entally retarded adults in the community are having children and are experiencing significant problems in parenting. Accurate fertility rates are unavailable and probably unobtainable, but the magnitude of the problem would seem to relate more to the service-intensive needs unique to each family rather than to any simple prevalence rate. As with other issues relevant to mental retardation, the level of intervention needed to have a positive impact on the situation seems to increase exponentially with the severity of the mental retardation. From the perspective of service needs, the situation of parents with mental retardation represents a major demand on all health and welfare service delivery systems. Mentally retarded parents in the community contribute more than a simple head count to the statistics for illiteracy, homelessness, child abuse, child neglect, failure to thrive, child sexual abuse, medical neglect, malnutrition, unemployment, and poverty.

Programming adjusted to meet the parenting deficiencies identified in mothers and fathers with mental retardation remains scarce. Existing programs have been able to help *some*

203

of these parents to successfully care for their preschool children. The complicating effects of certain personality types, psychiatric disorders, language disability, physical disabilities, poverty, too large family size, and absence of extended family support have left other parents with mental retardation less able to benefit from such programs. Experience with the limitations of parents with mental retardation shows that it is highly improbable that even with extensive support services they will ever be able to be adequate parents to school-age children and adolescents. When, furthermore, these children themselves exhibit various degrees of cognitive, language, emotional, and behavioral impairments, whether organic or environmental in etiology, then the possibility of parents with mental retardation effectively advocating for and participating in intervention programs for their children becomes effectively nil.

Before rushing to the conclusion that removal of the children with attendant termination of parental rights represents the only logical recourse when faced with such significant levels of parental cognitive limitation as have been described in this book, it may be helpful to alter the perspective by stepping back and viewing the problem in the broader context of human relationships. Alternative solutions may be generated by redefining the critical parameters. Many of the difficulties faced by persons with mental retardation, both in sheltered situations and in the community at large, center on society's tendency to objectify the needs, the interactions, and the people themselves. The issues of sex drives and the acceptance or rejection of sexuality in persons with mental retardation (objective aspect) drives out consideration of the needs to care and be cared for by others, to love and be loved by others, and to participate in a network of relationships that support the mentally retarded person's sense of self-worth (subjective aspect). Concern over the human drives to exhibit fertility and fecundity is then reduced to a series of scientific questions over contraceptive and abortive technologies. It is much easier to clarify technological choices than to decide on the appropriate frame of reference from which to approach normalization of persons who have mental retardation (Vanier, 1985). As attempts at normalization continually expand the range of options available to mentally retarded persons in the community, ultimately the remaining more limiting alternatives will mean that advocacy groups will be needed to reconsider those problematic areas in which the society at large is not itself normative. It would certainly not be reflective of modern American society to presume any significant consensus in issues related to sexuality and procreation. Indeed, the commercialized use of soft core and child pornography in advertising is frequently at distinct odds with what minimal community agreement there is. In this confused atmosphere there can be little rational discussion of the rights of parents with mental retardation to adopt or to have access to fertility technology.

The question with regard to the parenting problems of persons with mental retardation would seem to be not whether they should be parents but when. Obtaining aid through multiple agency interventions often produces a chaotic home situation that is far from optimal for normal child development. The ability of extended family support to obviate much of the negative impact of a parent with mental retardation (Spencer 1960) has received some validation from the case histories cited in this text. The possibilities of institutionalizing this support with extended group homes or with foster care placements for the mentally retarded parent/child dyad warrant further exploration.

The fundamental question has not been addressed. Attempts to answer it will only reveal an underlying polarization of basic philosophical orientation rather than contribute constructively to the situation of mentally retarded parents in the community. Is the fact that adults with significant mental retardation are having children an aberration, a sign of system failure, an index that current educational and community programs are unsuccessful? Or is this fact a logical, not unexpected, and not entirely undesirable outcome of normalization, and, in this latter context, would not all the difficulties associated with the situation of parents who have mental retardation be reflective of insufficient planning of support services? From a clinical perspective there are individual cases where it would seem that the latter context should be the appropriate perception. Further research on the impact on both parent and child of various situational parameters other than the degree of parental mental retardation as well as experimentation with alternate living arrangements would appear to be in order.

## REFERENCES

Spencer, E. (1960). *Light in the piazza*. New York: McGraw-Hill.
Vanier, J. (1985). *Man and woman he made them*. Mahwah, New Jersey: Paulist Press.

# Index